D1244959

SENIOR ADULT
MINISTRY
VOLUNTEER HANDBOOK

SENIOR ADULT
MINISTRY
VOLUNTEER HANDBOOK

Equipping You to Serve

Scripture quotations are taken from the Holy Bible, New International Version. Copyright © 1973, 1978, 1984, 2011 by Biblica, Inc.® Used by permission. All rights reserved worldwide.

First Edition: Year 2022
Senior Adult Ministry Volunteer Handbook / Outreach, Inc.
Paperback ISBN: 978-1-951304-90-4
eBook ISBN: 978-1-951304-91-1

CHURCHLEADERS
PRESS

Colorado Springs

SENIOR ADULT MINISTRY

VOLUNTEER HANDBOOK

Equipping You to Serve

Written by
Mikal Keefer

General Editor
Matt Lockhart

CHURCHLEADERS
PRESS

Colorado Springs

CONTENTS

INTRODUCTION

to the *Outreach Ministry Guides* Series

*Each of you should use whatever gift you have received to serve others, as
faithful stewards of God's grace in its various forms.*
(1 Peter 4:10)

*T*his handbook is part of a series designed to equip and empower church volunteers for effective ministry. If you're reading this, chances are you're a church volunteer. Thanks for your willingness to serve!

Several things make this handbook unique:
- The content is specific and practical for your given area of ministry.
- Experienced ministry practitioners—folks who've worked, served, and helped to train others in this particular area—compiled this information.
- It's written with you—a ministry volunteer—in mind.

Within these pages you'll find three sections. The first gives a brief overview of fundamental principles to provide you with a solid foundation for the ministry area in which you're serving.

Section 2 unpacks various skills related to the responsibilities involved. Understanding what is required and assessing if it's a good fit is helpful in creating a ministry team that is effective and serves together well.

Finally, Section 3 provides a multitude of practical ministry tools. These ideas and tips will help you demonstrate Jesus' love to the people you serve.

Whether you're a first-time volunteer or a seasoned veteran, my prayer is that the information and practical tools in this handbook will encourage and assist you. May God bless and guide you in your ministry!

—**Matt Lockhart,** Project Manager

to the *Senior Adult Ministry Volunteer Handbook*

$\mathcal{F}$irst, a confession: I'm a senior adult.

There's no one cheering louder for the success of your senior adult ministry than me. There's no better time than now for your ministry to meet the needs of people like me, too.

Most statistics are out of date the moment they're printed but trends (especially those that have held for decades) stay relevant. And here's a trend that shows no sign of changing course: We're living longer.

In the United States, the average lifespan in 1900 was 47.3 years. In 2000 it was 76.8 years. Today, an American can reasonably expect to tack about two years on to that total.[1] Elsewhere in the world the numbers vary, but the trend holds.

Which means your ministry to senior adults is not only important today, it will become even more important tomorrow, and the day after that. It's not just the number of senior adults that's skyrocketing. The diversity of people identifying as seniors is also expanding.

In your community spry 75-year-olds are holding their own on the tennis court, 52-year-old retirees are roofing houses for Habitat, and great-grandmothers are still in the workforce.

"Senior adult" no longer describes people who reach 65 and trade in their jobs for rocking chairs on the porch. It describes

---

1   https://www.cdc.gov/nchs/data/hus/2017/015.pdf

people who are both working and retired, in good health and poor, who are rich with purpose and who flounder for direction.

The training and tips you'll find in this little book will help you engage with and minister to the seniors in your church and community. You'll learn from people who've been at this awhile and discover what helps, what hurts, and how to avoid the mistakes they've made along the way.

So dig in.

But, before you do, a quick word of thanks.

Thank *you* for letting God use you to minister to and with seniors. We're a peculiar bunch and we know it. We live with an increasingly long list of aches and pains, we're sometimes prone to forgetfulness, and now and then we may test your patience.

But we need the connections you help us forge with one another, with our larger church family, and with God. You're helping and you're appreciated.

God bless you.

—**Mikal Keefer**, Author

SECTION 1

SENIOR ADULT MINISTRY FOUNDATIONS

CHAPTER 1

WHAT THE BIBLE SAYS ABOUT SENIOR ADULT MINISTRY

*N*ot much, actually—but it has a *lot* to say about seniors.

Consider these passages:

Stand up in the presence of the aged, show respect for the elderly and revere your God. I am the LORD.
(Leviticus 19:32)

In the same way, you who are younger, submit yourselves to your elders. All of you, clothe yourselves with humility toward one another, because, "God opposes the proud but shows favor to the humble." (1 Peter 5:5)

Honor your father and your mother, so that you may live long in the land the LORD your God is giving you.
(Exodus 20:12)

Listen to your father, who gave you life, and do not despise your mother when she is old. (Proverbs 23:22)

Is not wisdom found among the aged? Does not long life bring understanding? (Job 12:12)

No mention of Senior Saints potlucks appear in Scripture, but it's clear older adults are to be heard and valued, not overlooked or discarded. And for good reason: God seems to use them.

Among other older adults who played a significant role in the Bible are Adam, Enoch, Noah, Job, and Abram. Toss in Joseph, Moses, and Joshua and you've got a Who's Who of Bible luminaries, many of who accomplished amazing things deep into their old age.

Abram, for instance, was seventy-five when he left Haran. When Moses and Aaron stood before Pharaoh, demanding God's people be set free, Moses was eighty and Aaron eighty-three. Paul was in his sixties when he headed out on his final mission trip.

Caleb was forty when he scouted the Promised Land and eighty-five when he told Joshua he was ready to fight for and work the land he'd been promised there.

John was closing in on 90 when he wrote the Book of the Revelation and Noah was *six hundred* when the rain started falling. Quite the overachiever, that Noah.

Seniors haven't just been bystanders as God has rolled out his plans for humanity; they've been courageous, faithful participants.

It's true advanced age doesn't necessarily equal spiritual wisdom or even maturity. The world is full of older adults busy repeating the same mistakes they made in their twenties. But it's equally true those who walk with God for decades usually know him better than those who've just met him. They're better able to teach, offer counsel, and perhaps provide able leadership.

So even in our youth-focused culture, the church is to honor the elderly by treating them with respect and allowing them to continue contributing their skills, gifts, and talents. The Bible never hints at a retirement age for participation in service and worship—those are lifelong expectations in the Body of Christ.

Seniors aren't exempt—and most don't want to be.

And the Bible says to not only respect elders but, if there's a need, to provide for them as well. Consider:

Religion that God our Father accepts as pure and faultless is this: to look after orphans and widows in their distress and to keep oneself from being polluted by the world.
(James 1:27)

James specifically mentions widows as possibly requiring care. Widows who lacked resources in James' time had to rely on their extended families for support, or perhaps the support of adult sons. When those safety nets were missing, James urged the church to provide for widows' needs. Presumably many of the widows were older women whose poverty would have been extreme.

The need to financially support widows may have abated through the centuries, but it's not gone. Research launched by Horizon Investments found that more than 14% of American widows live beneath the poverty line and the older the widow the likelier health expenditures will worsen her situation.[2]

Finances aside, older widows and widowers often need help in other ways. Some are isolated or depressed. Others find physical infirmities make it impossible to do home maintenance or cope with tiny-screen technology. Old age can quickly limit eyesight, hearing, and movement.

Many widows remain isolated because there's no systematic effort to connect with them. Without a ministry focused on intentionally engaging widows, they can quickly fade into the background.

As your senior adult ministry serves older people, including widows, you'll do an amazing amount of good. To the seniors

2   Widows Are at Higher Risk of Falling Into Poverty, Horizon Investments, March 31, 2021.

who most need you, you're providing an emotional and spiritual lifeline. You're creating opportunities for meaningful fellowship and service.

You're doing what God asks you to do for people who are close to God's heart.

CHAPTER 2

WHY YOUR SENIOR ADULT MINISTRY MATTERS

*T*here are as many reasons your ministry matters as there are seniors whose lives you touch, but these three reasons are sufficient for your congregation to fully support your ministry efforts:

- You're meeting the needs of seniors in your congregation.
- You're attracting new seniors to your church.
- You're advocating for seniors and addressing unintentional ageism.

You're meeting the needs of seniors in your congregation

Think of it as "inreach," connecting with seniors already within the orbit of your church.

Some are easy to spot because they're often *at* church. They're active in worship services, participate in mission projects, and are up front teaching, preaching, or leading music. When you think "Pillars of the Church," these people come to mind.

Other seniors attend less frequently but are still visible. When you host a program that interests them they're there. Or they might snow-bird in Arizona half the year and worship with you only seasonally.

Some seniors may be off your radar altogether. They're homebound, in extended care facilities, or can no longer drive to church. Unless you do some looking, they're in the "out of sight, out of mind" camp.

Your ministry is a vital in staying connected to seniors and assessing their needs. Your pastor can't do it all and leaders in other ministries like youth, children, and missions have their own unique calling. Without your ministry, people will fall through the cracks.

You're able to attract new seniors to your church

Think of this as "outreach," letting the community know of programming for seniors that's relevant to older adults beyond your immediate congregation.

Chapters 10 and 12 suggest outreach programs that will snag attention of seniors in your community, drawing them through the doors of your church.

Don't believe the myth that older adults are already plugged into churches, or that they're all faithful believers. Studies (thank you, Barna Organization) indicate that while roughly 80% of older adults self-identify as Christian, less than 40% attend church monthly yet say their faith is very important in their lives,[3] which means the majority of seniors in your neighborhood are either unchurched or only loosely committed to their faith.

Your ministry isn't simply a caretaker ministry, hanging on to the seniors who are already on the church rolls. You're also an outreach ministry.

You're advocating for seniors

Nobody is deliberately excluding seniors from the life of your church. It just sort of happens.

"I volunteer in our children's ministry program," says Doug, who's nearly 70 and deals with herniated discs and arthritis in his back. "Last week our CE director called a 7:00 p.m. meeting at the church. I drove over in the dark to find the parking lot and walkways

---

3   A Snapshot of Faith Practices Across Age Groups, July 23, 2019 (https://www.barna.com/research/faithview-on-faith-practice).

were a skating rink courtesy of an ice storm. It wasn't safe for me to get into and out of the building so I turned around and left."

Another senior, Carol, struggles with the volume of Sunday morning services. "I wear hearing aids," she says. "The only way I can make out what's said from the stage is to have them in, but when the band starts playing it's actually painful. When I asked if maybe the music volume could be lowered I was told to bring earplugs."

So Carol has stopped attending services. "I can watch online later and at home I have a volume control," she says.

It might look like Doug and Carol are just being prickly old people—one complaining about nobody salting the sidewalk and the other complaining about music being too loud. But notice that both their concerns are based not on personal preferences but in biology: both are dealing with physical issues that are common in seniors.

As a senior adult ministry volunteer, one way your ministry matters is that you're there to advocate for seniors, to see your congregational life through their eyes. Is your building and parking lot safe for seniors? Are their physical limitations taken into consideration when planning church events? Are outreach efforts into the community aimed solely at young families or do they include seniors? Where in the church budget do you see dollars earmarked for resourcing seniors?

As a senior adult volunteer you're ideally positioned not just to advocate for seniors, but to also work proactively to uphold the value and dignity of older congregants. Ageism is prejudice against older people simply because of their age. It may be accepting negative stereotypes as factual ("Old people always complain") or dismissing older people as irrelevant, incapable, or hopelessly out of touch.

In the church it might look like this:

- Even though social issues are often considered from the pulpit, not once has dealing with ageism been addressed.

- You haven't sung one of the hymns your older people request in years, defaulting to music thought more attractive to younger congregants. Or, if you do pull out "The Old Rugged Cross," it's with new arrangement that lets your lead guitarist rock out.
- Your senior adult ministry has just completed an annual schedule (congratulations!) but no senior adults were consulted about programs and dates.
- A prevailing view that that older leader should step aside to make room for younger leaders.

Ageism lives best in shadows. Until someone points it out (you, perhaps?) it will continue. Don't assume your older adults will point it out; many older people have been socialized to not raise a ruckus.

A fourth reason your ministry matters: self-interest.

It may be impolite to talk about the church budget, but it's silly to ignore it. And if your church is like most, seniors make a significant contribution to covering the bills.

Pat Baker is a founding member of the National Presbyterian Older Adult Ministry Network and has served seniors for fifty years through both a government role and church positions. She's seen her share of seniors—and budgets.

"In mainline churches over fifty percent of the membership is older adults," says Baker. "That's across the board—Baptists, Presbyterians, Methodists, and other denominations. And when it comes to their budgets, most churches will tell you're they're supported more by older members than younger adults who are raising kids and paying for college." This means keeping your seniors engaged and participating in church (including the offerings) is no small thing.

Should money be a main motivator? Absolutely not, but a budget shortfall could be one consequence of ignoring the seniors your church. Other consequences are far more serious: seniors feeling distanced from the faith community they desperately need, a lack of compassion for the elderly being unintentionally reinforced in your church, and failure to fulfill the Biblical expectation that senior adults will be cherished, not ignored.

Your ministry matters, and *you* matter as you serve in it. God is using you in ways you'll likely never know this side of heaven. Every contact you have with a senior is a lifeline of love.

CHAPTER 3

QUALITIES OF AN EFFECTIVE SENIOR ADULT MINISTRY

*W*hen it comes to effective Senior Adult Ministries, one size does not fit all. One church might have a vibrant, engaged senior Sunday school class while across the street another congregation can't get older adults to class no matter how many free donuts are dangled as bait. An effective ministry might look like lunch on Tuesday at the local pancake house. Or a short-term mission trip to Guatemala. Or exercise classes three times a week in the church all-purpose room.

As varied as senior ministries appear, those with lasting impact have a few things in common that form the foundation of any effective senior ministry—including yours. So pause to look at what you're actually doing—do you see these foundations in place?

If not, find a way to install them before your ministry collapses.

Effective adult senior ministries are Jesus-Centered

There are dozens of adult social societies, fraternal organizations, and sororities. Most do fine work and encourage generous behavior but aren't really *ministries* because they aren't centered on Jesus.

A Jesus-centered ministry is one where Jesus is at the heart of everything that happens. He's talked about, talked with, and you measure success not by how many outings your seniors take but whether they're growing spiritually.

You'll know your ministry is likely Jesus-centered when you see the following:

- **You talk about Jesus (and God)—a lot.** In devotions, Bible studies, and casual conversations his name comes up and your group members intentionally seek to know him. The curriculum you choose is less about character development and more about Jesus. The service you provide is done in his name. There's an element of evangelistic outreach in your ministry that proclaims Jesus.
- **You pray often.** You pray for and with one another. Doing so invites Jesus into your relationships and circumstances.
- **You see kindness and compassion.** When people are connected to Jesus it shows through transformed lives. One such transformation—actually a fruit of the Spirit—is a sense of loving compassion. Do you see it?

Effective senior ministries provide purpose

Some senior adults experience a loss of purpose as they age. They may have lost a meaningful career or beloved spouse. They're no longer raising children and health issues limit their ability to engage fully in activities they once enjoyed.

They start wondering: Why are they getting out of bed each day?

An effective senior ministry helps fuel a sense of purpose by providing relational opportunities, service opportunities, and an awareness of where your seniors fit in the body of Christ. You'll help seniors see they have something to contribute, a story to tell, and a Savior to lift up. They'll glimpse a vision for something beyond themselves.

Effective senior ministries promote spiritual growth

Effective ministries center their activities around faith development and devote time and effort to strengthening spiritual connections. In later chapters you'll find a treasure trove of activities to help that happen, but almost any activity can be useful if you intentionally make spiritual connections.

Don't see how that's possible? Okay: how is bowling backwards like trusting God? You're acting on faith, that's how. See? Case closed.

Effective senior ministries are encouraging

Approaching your seniors with respect may seem like a small thing but it's huge to seniors who feel increasingly diminished by life. How are you honoring your seniors? What words and activities feed their sense of self-worth? How are you regularly communicating God's love for them?

Effective ministries have an upbeat feel, a positivity that's refreshing to senior adults who may be living long, drab days. How would you describe the emotional tenor of your ministry?

Effective adult senior ministries provide support

Your ministry can't do everything for everyone but there's a Biblical expectation that your church—and ministry—will help older believers in need. That need may show up in several areas:

• **Physical needs** range from simple things like providing a ride to church to something more challenging like cleaning out gutters. What, if anything, can you do? How can you match able-bodied volunteers (hello, youth group) with specific seniors' needs?

• **Social needs** can be met with a check-in phone call, a home visit, or an officially sanctioned Skip-Bo night in the church basement.

• **Mental health needs** might be met with a phone call to discuss current events or sitting with a senior and looking through photo albums, inviting stories about the people and places you find there.

• **Financial needs** are trickier—there's clearly a limit on what you can do. But no senior should face an empty pantry; a food delivery can be healthy and heartening.

• **Spiritual needs** are your ministry's primary calling, and one you're fulfilling already. In the rest of this book you will see how others who are ministering to seniors approach meeting this need.

The foundations of your ministry aren't complicated and are likely the foundation of your church itself. Keeping Christ central and lifted up, providing purpose and spiritual growth, serving and encouraging others, growing in a friendship with Jesus and gratefully serving others.

No wonder the seniors in your church are hungry for what you and your ministry offer—you're doing the work of Christ.

And here's a bonus fun fact:

Among adult social clubs are the Elks, Moose, Eagles, Woodchucks, Owls, Orioles, Beavers, and Buffaloes (but so far no Wombats). So if you do decide to start a club, *Wombats* is available.

SECTION 2

THE ANATOMY OF AN EFFECTIVE
SENIOR ADULT MINISTRY

CHAPTER 4

MODELS OF SENIOR ADULT MINISTRY

*O*ne strength of your ministry is that it doesn't have to follow any rigid pattern. It can shift with the needs of the seniors you serve, along with the talents and gifts of the volunteers who serve in the ministry.

If the leadership of your church or ministry has established an approach for senior adult ministry, that's the way to go. We're in no way suggesting you stage a coup and take your ministry off in an entirely new direction.

But looking through other ways to meet the needs of seniors might spark an idea that you could incorporate—after discussing it with your leadership, of course.

Following are nine ministry models working in churches. They're all good, but each requires a decision: will you minister *to* seniors, *with* seniors, or do both?

A ministry *to* seniors puts seniors on the receiving end of ministry efforts. They aren't involved in actually doing ministry.

A ministry *with* seniors involves seniors in the planning and delivery of ministry. They're active participants on the ministry team, both serving and being served as needs dictate.

The latter approach has much to offer seniors—make it your goal to have seniors serving each other in the following ministry models:

The Sunday school model

This approach will be discussed in detail later, but for now, hear this: the rumor that all Senior Sunday school classes are dead isn't true. What *is* true is that Senior classes must be relevant to thrive. You have to give seniors good reasons to attend. Study topics must be applicable to seniors' lives and make room for both study and relationship.

Here's a glimpse at a Chapter 7: senior Sunday school has a relational aspect that will likely meet the strongest felt need.

The Bible study model

A Bible study ministry appeals to lifelong learners who want to better understand Scripture.

The Bible study may take place in a Sunday school class, but it may also take the form of a separate study series. This model generally works best if you have a trained theologian handling the teaching.

The study may last for several meetings or several months. If you live near a Bible College, ask for a syllabus and see what classes first-year students take. In fact, find out if the College might have a grad student or other well-trained person who'd do a six-part New Testament Survey class or a series on how to interpret the Bible (Hermeneutics) for free or a small stipend. When a church in Michigan asked a nearby Bible college for help, an upperclassman came to lead the class in exchange for college credit. A win-win!

Bible studies generally have a greater focus on covering content than encouraging fellowship, so don't limit yourself to a steady diet of only Bible studies. Seniors crave connections, too.

The enrichment programs model

This is a Bible study's less-biblical cousin. Rather than tackle a Bible topic, put together a series of topical presentations such as "How to Exercise Safely," "Staying Safe While Traveling," or "How to Connect With Long Distance Grandkids."

How is this Jesus-centered, you're asking—and you're right to do so. Hold these sessions at times community members can attend and advertise the programs widely. Briefly explain before each presentation who you are and what motivates you: You're facilitating the meeting because it's a way of sharing the love of Christ.

Ask seniors to serve refreshments and strike up conversations. Reach out to any and all who come to the events, including first-time visitors.

And here's a plus: You don't have to create the enrichment programs yourself. Contact your local Council on Aging and other government agencies who serve the elderly to see what programs they're willing to present. Nearly always there's no charge, and agencies are eager to find new ways to reach into the community.

The small group model

A small group for seniors is an ideal spot for friendships to form because of the relational nature of small groups. Some senior ministries organize "dinner parties" where groups of four to eight seniors meet for meals in one another's houses. Others have found success with film nights that include viewing a movie in homes and then debriefing it over coffee.

And some small groups are of the traditional prayer, Bible study, and discussion variety.

Experiment to see what kind of small group your seniors would prefer.

The relational model

This approach emphasizes conversation and connections. Often there's a topic presented each week ("Challenges of Aging," "Finding Hope," "Dealing with Loss," "Surprises in the Seventies," for instance) with a brief devotion and then extensive discussion.

Other relational groups pull out board games, play card games, hike trails, or try new restaurants together. Whatever the activity, be sure group members can do it while chatting.

If you choose to emphasize socializing, keep your meeting Jesus-centered by including prayer and, perhaps, a very brief devotional thought.

The congregational care model

This sort of ministry focuses on connecting with seniors (and others, as well) who need a level of pastoral care that can be delivered by lay people like most of your seniors.

At First United Methodist Church in Cookeville, Tennessee, Jess Welch coordinates visits to church members who could benefit from having a friendly, caring face come to their home, hospital room, or assisted living facility. Many of those who receive visits are elderly.

"Visits keep those who can't come to church in fellowship with our church family," says Welch. "We're also able to evaluate whether additional ministry is needed, such as a visit from a pastor."

Seniors are often ideal candidates to visit other seniors. Welch offers training but says what's most needed is "compassion and a willingness to listen. Those go a very long way in caring for others."

If your existing senior adult ministry doesn't have a care component in it, how might adding it to your group be beneficial? No professional credentials are needed to provide this level of emotional and spiritual support and training is available at a minimal cost. See Chapter 23 for sources.

The mission and service model

Do you think seniors are too feeble to get involved in service projects?

Think again.

You'll find a long list of service projects in Chapter 12 suitable for a variety of seniors, from those who are bed-ridden (pray through congregational prayer requests and organize a prayer chain) through seniors with unlimited energy (volunteer at an after-school program for children).

Research confirms that investing in others and looking past one's own challenges to help others brings happiness. Plugging seniors into service is a service to your seniors.

What service projects might you add to your existing senior adult ministry?

The support group model

This approach to senior adult ministry is, by design, open to all seniors so offer it in combination with a more accessible model.

A support group is a facilitated discussion that brings together people who have shared a common, often difficult, experience. A relatively sophisticated understanding of group dynamics is required, so it's best if a social worker or mental health professional leads the group.

Support groups exist for cancer survivors, those experiencing grief, widows and widowers, grandparents raising grandkids, caregivers, those dealing with drug or alcohol addiction: the list is as long as the challenges seniors face.

Be aware that announcing the existence of a support group will open it up beyond just your seniors—and that's a positive. It's often comforting to see you're not alone, and that an issue can impact people of all ages.

The intergenerational model

You know what can really perk up a senior adult ministry?

Including people who aren't senior adults.

Churches generally silo members based on their age or life stage. Parents of young children go to class with other parents of young children. Kids are with kids, youth with youth, and seniors with seniors.

There's value in creating silos: People of the same generation have a lot in common. The problems they face are often similar. They have the same cultural influences. They "get" one another.

But if you at least occasionally mix things up, good things can happen.

Dick and Karen were visiting friends and attended church with them in Stillwater, Oklahoma. When they arrived, they discovered the college and older adult classes were meeting together.

"We walked into a room full of round tables and were told we could sit anywhere, but there had to be both college students and older adults at each table," says Dick.

The couple had wandered into a six-week experiment: If seniors and young adults were given the chance to talk about spiritual matters what might they teach each other? The results were dramatic.

"We showed up for week five of six," says Karen. "The conversations at our table were relaxed and quickly dove deep. And there was already talk of extending the experiment—these very different people were becoming fast friends."

There was dynamic back-and-forth, everyone contributing to the table conversations. Both collegians and seniors had something to teach—and learn.

"We were only there one Sunday," says Dick. "We wished we could have gone again."

"Intergenerational" really isn't a model—it's a method, a way to give your ministry a shot of energy and open up fresh perspectives. It's also a way for isolated seniors to make younger friends.

And it's a vivid depiction of what it means to be the body of Christ.

Your senior adult ministry probably incorporates elements of several of the models described above. That's fine. Or it may include a model that isn't even described, and that's okay, too.

Prayerfully ask God which models will best fit your situation. Talk with seniors and see what they have to say. And be aware that your ministry is fluid: a model that works today may no longer work in a year or two. Always be open to new ideas, new approaches. Remember, you're in this to do ministry, not establish traditions.

CHAPTER 5

SORTING OUT THE SENIORS

*H*ere's a little insight about seniors courtesy of the World Health Organization:

By 2030, 1 in 6 people on the planet will be age 60 or older. That means there will be roughly 1.4 billion seniors and, by 2050, that number will double. In some countries the aging population has already reached record levels—in Japan 30 percent of the population is over 60 years old.[4]

Granted, there aren't a billion seniors currently involved in your ministry. But you have *some* seniors, and the potential for more showing up is enormous. If you want to be ready when the Lord sends more your way, you've got to figure out who qualifies as a senior, who the seniors are in your church, and how to effectively engage seniors.

Who exactly is a senior?

The leadership of your ministry may have quantified who's invited to join the Senior Sunday school class or the Seniors' luncheon. Some churches use age as the measurement, declaring you're a senior at 50, 55, or 60 years of age.

Other churches leave the minimum age vague. If you feel like a senior, you're a senior. No ID is checked at the door.

---

4   *Consultation on Global Strategy and action Plan on Ageing and Health*, World Health Organization, October 2021.

Whatever decisions have been made about who qualifies as a senior, you need to know the score. These are the people you're committed to serving, so knowing who fits your ministry profile is key.

Who exactly are the seniors *in your church*?

Ask your ministry leadership for a list of seniors in your congregation or, if no list exists, create one. Include people you see and also seniors who aren't visible because they're homebound or just occasional attenders.

Use that list to pray for the people on it—and add names as new folks who fit the profile enter your church.

Pay special attention to the seniors with whom you work directly. If you're a small group leader, it's the members of your group. If you lead a meeting, they're the seniors filling the chairs. If you're on a visitation team, they're the seniors whose doorbells you ring.

And how exactly do you engage seniors?

We'll dive into the deep end of that pool in later chapters but first there's someone you should meet.

Pat Baker has discovered an effective way to define who fits into her senior adult ministry and at the same time engage a wide variety of seniors. It's simple, brilliant, and she's willing to share.

"I don't put an age on anything I do for seniors," she says. "I just say it's for adults. If it's a lunch in the middle of the day or a trip in the middle of the week it will be older, retired people who show up—though there are people in their 50's who take part in activities."

Pat adheres to the "you're a senior if you think you're a senior" school of ministry and has seen it work well. There's no secret handshake to learn or minimum age requirement. You just show up and participate, which means her ministry includes people from their mid-50's through their late 80's.

And when it comes to providing programming to engage those seniors, she approaches it this way:

"I don't use the terminology out loud and it didn't originate with me," Pat says, "But when I think about older adults I don't look at them chronologically. Instead I mentally sort them into three groups: The *Go-Go's*, the *Slow-Go's*, and the *No-Go's*.

"Go-Go's are older adults who, no matter their age, are still working, are active in the community and church, and who often have family living nearby who are a regular part of their lives. The last thing Go-Go's are interested in is going to lunch with a bunch of seniors.

"Slow-Go's have started to slow down some because of health issues or because they themselves are caregivers (they're supporting other people in their families).

"Then there are the No-Go's. They can no longer come to church and may feel they've been forgotten. These older people are the least visible and most vulnerable, yet still want to be part of the church."

Rather than segment the three groups Pat provides activities and programs appropriate for each on her larger roster of programming, letting seniors pick and choose where to plug in.

This approach means you can't let your ministry be one-dimensional. If your entire ministry is a series of meetings in the church building it eliminates the No-Go's who can't possibly attend. And depending on when you schedule meetings, the Slow-Go's and Go-Go's who are still employed can't show up.

Because it's nearly impossible to create a program that meets the situational needs of all three groups, why not offer a buffet of activities right-sized for each group and let your seniors sort themselves out?

Doing so creates a ministry where everyone's involved, and everyone can also serve.

There's significant ministry each group of seniors can do. No-Go's may be homebound, but they're often fierce prayer warriors. They can phone other seniors who are isolated, providing encouragement and socialization.

Slow-Go's can often do whatever a Go-Go can do, just at a slower pace. And while they're often busy serving as caregivers for older or younger family members, they're looking for opportunities to somehow plug in.

And those Go-Go's zooming around can be valuable helpers in your ministry.

"It's not unusual for Go-Go's to attend our events for seniors not as seniors, but as volunteers helping pull off the events," says Baker. "They just aren't yet ready to see themselves as truly elderly."

So when it comes to sorting out your seniors, here are a few take-aways:

- Find out if your leadership has a definition of "senior."
- Find out who in your congregation fits the description.
- Pray for your seniors—those who attend and those who don't.
- Include activities in your ministry appropriate for Go-Go's, Slow-Go's, and No-Go's.
- Consider not advertising your activities as "for seniors" and instead positioning them as "for adults."
- Stand back and watch God work.

CHAPTER 6

QUALITIES OF EFFECTIVE SENIOR ADULT MINISTRY VOLUNTEERS

*H*opefully you have a job description provided by your ministry leaders. If not, see Chapter 21 for a document that can assist in creating one. Nailing down a job description helps you know what to do.

But let's talk here not about what you'll *do*, but about who you *are*.

The qualities, values, skills, and commitment you bring to your ministry role is more important than the to-do list a job description provides. Why? Because as you do ministry with senior adults you'll discover your job description could only anticipate so much; endless situations will arise that require you to trust God and make decisions on the spot.

Mark, a ministry worker in Colorado, recalls a time he'd finally carved out a day to write the material he'd be presenting on senior adult ministry. "It was do or die time," Mark says, "Time to pull the material together or else."

But then Mark got an email from a senior friend asking for a ride to a doctor's appointment. "John's cancer was back and his oncologist wanted to go over the results of John's recent PET scan. When a doctor insists on delivering the news in person that's not an appointment you want to miss," recalls Mark.

The doctor's office was 70 miles away and John was too weak to make the drive himself. "I remember thinking, 'What terrible timing. I really need this day to write about serving seniors.' And then it struck me: I needed to serve *this* senior. He needed me not just for the ride, but to debrief the news as we drove home."

Mark's job description probably favored his completing his work but Mark's values insisted he serve first and pull an all-nighter later to complete the project.

In your role as a volunteer you'll see needs and have to decide if you can meet them. You'll hear a comment and realize there's a further conversation required. You'll sense a nudge from the Lord and have to decide whether to follow or deflect.

Who you are will determine what happens next. Who are you, and how willing you are to let Jesus transform and lead you?

So let's look at the qualities and values that can shape your effective ministry to senior adults. Will everything that follows describe you? No—at least not all the time. But as you prayerfully ask God to work in and through you, you'll be amazed at how you grow and how your heart opens to senior adults.

To be an effective volunteer in senior adult ministry, it's best if:

You like older people

"It may seem obvious, but you've got to enjoy seniors," says Pat Baker. "You've got to enjoy hearing their stories—sometimes the same stories again and again."

And like means *like*, not tolerate. No one appreciates being treated like a mission field or processed like a chore on a checklist. Seniors (like everyone) want to spend time with people who sincerely enjoy being with them.

So, on a one to ten scale, how much do you enjoy being with seniors?

You're a believer

Anyone can befriend the elderly but if you want to do ministry— to love others as Jesus loves them—you've got to know Jesus and know him well. He's the One who fuels the insight, compassion, and love that will make you effective in serving seniors.

As a volunteer in senior adult ministry your spiritual condition matters. You're dealing with people who often need hope, hope you can't provide if you don't have it yourself.

So consider: is your friendship with Jesus growing, going, or somewhere in between? How ready are you to share what you know to be true?

You're a person of prayer

You're not in this ministry thing alone, you know.

If Jesus has called you into this he's looking to encourage and equip you. He's your partner in this endeavor and partners need to stay connected. One way is to pray—frequently and honestly.

"Frequently" and "honestly." How well do those words describe your prayer life?

You know the Bible

No, you don't need to memorize the whole thing. But you do need to know the story laid out in Scripture: how people seem determined to sin and how God has responded with love, paving a road home to himself through the death and resurrection of Jesus.

And it's good to know portions of the Bible that speak to issues faced by seniors, especially issues that prompt fear or despair.

Your reassurance will always be welcome, but there's far more comfort when you can point people to the reassurance spelled out in the Word of God.

See Chapter 14 for a cheat sheet of passages you'll want to know.

You're patient

Seniors can be, well, slow.

Slow to speak, slow to move, slow to make connections or embrace change. They're often not fans of new homes, new programs, new processes.

That's not all seniors, of course, but enough that you'll find your patience stretched thin at times, and that has to be okay because you can't change those seniors.

You can only love them. Sometimes love is spelled "patience."

You're a championship listener

Most people (ministry volunteers like you included) have never been trained how to listen well. We just sort of assume it comes naturally to us—and we may be wrong.

In Chapter 15 you'll get down-and-dirty training on how to listen well and to *look* like you're listening so seniors feel seen and heard. Listening is one of the best ways you can minister to people who sometimes feel invisible, so don't skip that chapter!

You keep getting training

There's this book, of course, plus a stack of resources listed in Chapter 23. That's one kind of training.

The other kind—and it's important, too—is being mentored by people who've served in this ministry longer than you have.

You are now deputized to find a mentor.

Ask your ministry leader or pastor if you can tag along on a few home visits or meetings with seniors. Take an online course or phone another church with a senior adult ministry to see what you can learn from them.

Invest in sharpening your skills and deepening your effectiveness.

You express warmth

It can be a cold world when you're elderly. You may face days with very little in them, especially on the relational front. You'd love to get a ten-minute "just rang because I was thinking of you, what's up?" call. You'd love to get a hug. You're hungry for connection.

Check with your leader about handing out hugs, but it's almost always okay to place your hand on the hand of a senior you're visiting when you pray for him or her. And it's absolutely always fine to project warmth through a smile, the tone of your voice, and your sincere care.

Ask people who know you well: Do I seem warm and inviting? What would help me be more so?

You treat seniors with respect

Many seniors share the experience of a 70-year-old by the name of Dale: they're patronized and dismissed because people don't take an interest in their backstory.

Dale retired as a full partner at a national accounting firm. Along the way in his career he advised the Securities and Exchange Commission, served on enough national boards to build a house, and was an expert witness in complicated fraud cases. He's an accountant's accountant and has stayed current with the law and emerging accounting techniques.

But when he volunteered to review his church's books after it became clear they were in shambles, Dale didn't expect to hear that a younger person should probably tackle the job. The tiny print and all, he was told. The church was asking a recent college graduate with a business degree to take a look.

"That's fine," says Dale. "But nobody was interested in hearing about my credentials and I was dismissed out of hand because of my age. Assuming that age equals incompetence is crazy."

Crazy, indeed.

Your success in ministry depends on avoiding assumptions about seniors. Give seniors the courtesy of respect.

You show empathy

Unless you're a senior yourself you probably don't know what it's like to find that everything aches when you carefully creak out of bed in the morning. Or how it feels when your grandkids ignore you or your spouse of 40 years is lost to cancer.

But you can empathize with seniors who do know.

Empathy—the ability to understand and share the feelings of others—is a ministry essential. It's a blend of noticing body language, tonal inflections, withholding judgement, listening well, and experience.

Add compassion to the mix, too, because empathy is powered by a deep desire to express care through understanding another person's feelings and perspective.

Given that description, how empathic would you say you are? How do you show empathy? How could you gain more experience being empathic?

You're a careful communicator

Seniors often experience hearing loss so your enunciation and attention to volume is important. When addressing older seniors check to see if your volume is okay. If it is, no big deal. If it isn't, you'll know and can adjust accordingly.

And if you happen to have facial hair, a note: One ministry volunteer shaved off an impressive handlebar moustache so hard-of-hearing seniors could better understand him since they could see his lips.

Be like that guy. Don't let anything get in the way of communicating clearly.

You're comfortable discussing death

Older adults find death a difficult topic to avoid. They likely have peers with terminal conditions or who have died. Death is in sharper focus for seniors.

Good news: Because of Jesus you have good news to share about death. It's not the end, but knowing that doesn't make the *process* of dying more attractive. So get ready to talk about dying. Know what the Bible says and what you believe. Settling the issue in your own heart and mind prepares you to engage with others.

You've set boundaries

Your ministry leader can help you here, so ask about it.

As a trusted person in the lives of seniors you may be asked to have a medical power of attorney, or to be the executor of a will. Can you really handle that?

Are you willing to run errands, take phone calls at midnight, shovel snow or mow yards? You're called to serve, but somewhere there's an outer limit of what you can deliver. And you don't want to promise what you can't or won't deliver.

Decide on your boundaries now, before you're forced to do so on the spot. Ask Jesus where he'd set them and then serve within them joyfully.

You know local resources

Who in your local government helps seniors in need? Who provides transportation, assures a supply of healthy food, can set up a low-cost eye exam? It's probably not your senior adult ministry, but you can make calls on behalf of seniors who need help that's beyond the scope of your ministry.

Start with the local Council on Aging and network from there. Check with a local crisis center that likely has referral information. Get the numbers, write them down, and carry them with you so you're ready to make a referral on the spot.

Jesus works through secular agencies, too.

You're courageous

You may sit with a weeping widow or hear about tumors or face someone who's furious with God and—by extension—you. You may have to leave your comfort zone so far behind you can't even see it in the rear-view mirror.

Are you willing to go where seniors' needs take you? Where Jesus is calling you to go?

You can live with silence

Sometimes a lonely senior will simply want you to be present, to quietly be present with her. She doesn't want to hear a sermon and doesn't have the energy for a dynamic conversation.

Nancy's mother is in an assisted living facility. After visiting her mother Nancy stops by the lounge where there are usually several widows sitting alone. She slides in beside one and gently asks, "Can I sit with you awhile?"

She's seldom shooed away, but often there's little or no conversation. "I know the person I'm with is thinking about her life. She's deep in her memories," says Nancy. "So I just quietly bear witness. That's enough.

"Some of my best conversations with older people haven't involved words," says Nancy.

You can deal with the smells

A small thing right up to the moment it isn't: How well can you deal with that hospital and nursing home smell?

You know the one. It's a combination of industrial cleaning compounds, bodily odor, and stale air—and it turns some peoples' stomachs.

Volunteer in senior adult ministry long enough and you'll encounter that smell. If it's something you absolutely can't handle let your ministry leader know you're not cut out for senior visitation in some settings.

You keep first things first

Your goal is to bring seniors deeper into a friendship with Jesus.

Don't let that message get lost as you create a schedule of programs and activities. Day trips to the art museum are wonderful, but unless you make a spiritual connection you've wasted the day.

Always be asking Jesus, "What do you want to make of this moment?"

SECTION 3

SENIOR ADULT MINISTRY
IDEAS, TIPS, AND TOOLS

CHAPTER 7

15 IDEAS TO ENERGIZE SUNDAY SCHOOL FOR SENIORS

*T*he most engaging senior adult Sunday school classes are those that deal with topics the seniors actually want to tackle.

It's fine to walk through a specific book of the Bible in your class, but let's be honest: There's probably very little your seniors haven't heard before. If they're 68 and in Sunday school, odds are they've been attending Sunday school since they were six *or* eight. They know how the story of David and Goliath will end and nobody is rooting for the giant.

So if they're not coming for new information or for your riveting teaching (sorry), why should they show up each week? And if most of your seniors aren't showing up at all, what might prompt them to do so?

Three things:

1. Fellowship
2. Spiritual hunger
3. More fellowship

Fellowship in senior adult Sunday school classes

Fellowship—coming together to pray, talk, and engage with faith—meets a need shared by many seniors who live increasingly isolated lives. The Bible lesson is important, but it may not be the prime motivation for seniors to come to Sunday school.

Encouraging fellowship isn't complicated: just make room for seniors to form and enjoy friendships. Ask open-ended questions that prompt discussion in class. Don't view the coffee-and-donut conversations before class as wasted time—it may be the richest part of the class hour.

If you've seen Sunday school as a place to do religious education, you're not wrong. But your seniors have dozens of places they can access religious education. Books, podcasts, television shows, radio, magazines—there's an avalanche of information out there.

But fellowship? Connecting with other believers to share life together? That's rare in the lives of many seniors—so make Sunday school a place it happens through casual conversation and small group discussions. Help seniors connect—that's oxygen to lonely seniors and enriching to already-connected seniors.

Spiritual hunger in Senior Adults

Growing older has a way of prompting seniors to ponder big, hard questions: What's my purpose now that I'm not working? What happens after death? Why hasn't God fixed what's broken in my kids or grandkids? Where can I find lasting comfort?

Seniors not only find the big questions intriguing, they have time to engage with those questions. Some seniors are open to God in ways they've never been open before.

And that's an opportunity for you. Grappling with big questions keeps your Sunday school class relevant, fresh, and satisfies spiritual hunger. It answers questions your seniors are actually asking—or would ask if they thought it was safe to do so.

So, survey your seniors to find out what questions they have. Were they creating the curriculum, what would they make sure was covered? Finding lessons that explore what the Bible says about burning questions gives your class a shot of adrenaline, firing up both interest and attendance.

Here are 15 more ways to bring a fading senior adult Sunday school class back to life:

1. Mix it up (a bit)

Senior adults tend to appreciate predictability, but nobody likes being bored. Mixing relevant, one-off topical studies in with your regular curriculum is a way to give your class ongoing appeal.

Plus, topical studies give you a reason to connect with non-attending seniors to tell them about upcoming topics. Be clear you'll welcome them for just a topical study but the invitation is there to plug in on a weekly basis, too.

2. Go intergenerational

At least for a brief time do what the church in Oklahoma did: combine classes with another age-group and encourage conversation in small groups.

This works best with topical lessons that are application oriented rather than a doctrinal lesson or Bible-fact lesson. "Paul's First Missionary Journey" doesn't give much space for discussion, but "How To Share Your Faith Effectively" or "Is There Really Joy in Jesus?" lessons make for intriguing sharing among generations.

3. Less lecture, more discussion

If you're doing all the talking in your class, that's probably a problem. There's a place for lectures but a steady diet casts your seniors as observers, not participants.

When selecting curriculum pick lessons that include open-ended questions. Those are questions that can't be answered with a simple "yes" or "no," or by reciting a fact from the lecture. Open-ended questions pull seniors into discussions.

4. Take attendance in stealth mode

Be subtle, but keep a record of who's in class and who isn't. Why? You'll know to follow up if a senior disappears for two or three weeks. Is that person sick or homebound? Is there a way you can help the absentee senior? You won't know to ask if you don't keep track of who's attending.

Long-weekend get-aways, family visits, business trips, and the like mean you'll be lucky to see class members two or three times a month, and that's okay. But if someone disappears altogether it's time to investigate.

By the way, never try to shame people into attending more frequently. Instead, give them irresistible reasons to attend as often as possible.

5. Freshen up the room

Many Sunday school classes meet in windowless church basements that were last painted in 1973. Brighten things up with a cheerful coat of paint and by adding more lighting. Move around the chairs to form discussion clusters. Have music playing as seniors enter the room.

It doesn't take much to add a little energy to your environment.

6. Change the venue

Maybe not permanently, but occasionally and, hopefully, for a purpose.

If you're teaching about the lilies of the field, could you meet on the church lawn near flower beds? How about meeting in unusual spaces in or around your building that connect somehow to the lesson? Be sure those one-off spaces are safe and accessible for seniors who have mobility challenges.

7. Share the music stand

If you have capable class members, ask them to lead lessons now and then. Sharing upfront time builds ownership in the class and adds variety.

If you're the only one speaking from behind that music stand up front, ask God who else could do a good job. You may need to mentor other leaders, but that's part of equipping the saints to do ministry.

8. Watch your language

Instead of calling your class "Sunday school," describe it as a "Fellowship" or "Spiritual Discovery Hour." Use anything except "school" because when people hear that term they make assumptions, sometimes negative ones.

Weed out school terminology, too. Don't describe yourself as the teacher; you're the facilitator or leader. Avoid words like "lesson plan," "study," and "classroom." Yes, it will be awkward awhile, but you'll find that seniors would much rather think of themselves as lifelong learners than Sunday school students.

And if your group's name is something cute such as Senior Saints, Senior Sages, Golden Oldies, Young-at-Hearts, or Power Hour-ers, ask your class if that's *really* how they want to be known.

Let the group suggest something new or designate a few seniors to meet and come back with ideas.

9. Relaunch your class

If a marketing company was to describe your class, what words would it use? Unfortunately, many classes feel tired, repetitive, and predictable.

You can revitalize your class with a relaunch so long as you've made changes you can talk about. A relaunch may well give seniors who've decided to not come a reason to reconsider.

10. Shorten lessons

Just because you've got an hour doesn't need you need to use it all.

People in general have shorter attention spans than they had a generation ago, and seniors in particular may have difficulty focusing for extended periods.

Here's what that means to you: be generous with the coffee-and-donut portion of your hour and cut the actual lesson time a bit. Take it as a personal challenge to get your lesson's message across in 30 instead of 50 minutes.

Also, post a conversation starter so seniors see it coming into the room. It gives shy seniors a launch pad to initiate a discussion.

Following are ten potential starters:

- Describe what life was like for you when you were 21.
- What was your first pet's name? How did you feel about the pet?
- If you have grandkids, say a little something about them.
- What was Christmas morning like when you were a child?
- What's your favorite sort of music? Why that style?
- Who's someone famous you've either met or would like to meet?
- If you could give a piece of advice to teenagers today, what would it be?
- What's a lesson you learned you'll never forget? How did you learn it?
- Your first car: what was it, how did you get it, and what became of it?
- What's a question you'd ask God if you knew you'd get a direct answer?

11. Shorten series, too

Most lesson books come with 13 lessons. That's a quarter of curriculum in the publishing world. Yet, seniors may tire of a subject before 13 weeks drag by.

Make your class more dynamic by limiting series to 4-6 weeks. Curriculum publishers do provide those resources and, if you can't find them, pull the 4-6 best lessons out of a longer, quarterly book.

12. Ask for commitment and discipleship

Too often we shy away from asking people to commit to attendance, application, or anything else. We're just grateful they showed up.

But seniors are growing in their faith, too Help them do that by incorporating discipleship into your class. Give your seniors a solid foundation in how to read and understand the Bible, pray specifically and with intention, and give of themselves in meaningful ways. Don't assume your seniors are especially holy because of their years in the church; there will be places they need to grow, too.

When you ask for dedication and commitment, you help seniors see themselves as truly connected to the class, to God, and to other seniors on the same journey.

13. Flip the formula

When picking curriculum, rather than start by selecting content and then moving to practical application, flip it.

Ask seniors what they need to know or do and then start where your seniors actually are in life. If they're struggling with finances deal with what the Bible says about money. If they're feeling lonely, dive into what the Bible says about God's abiding love for us.

It's okay to teach a "how to" class about friendship, finances, fellowship, or almost anything else. You stay relevant and scratch real itches in the lives of your seniors.

14. As a class, do ministry together

Not everyone can do everything, but what if you took on projects that were within reach for most or all of your seniors?

You'll find a range of service projects in Chapter 12. Tell your class you're conducting an experiment to see what you can all learn by tackling one of the projects.

Plan to do it, do it, and then debrief: How did it go? What did you learn? Do you want to do something like this again? What skills or information does the class want before taking on another project?

15. Have fun

If you're leading the class ask yourself this: Are you having fun? If so, does it show? And on a scale of one to ten, how much fun are class members having? Is there laughter or is everyone too busy taking notes?

Energy in a class is contagious and if you aren't enthused it's unlikely anyone else will be, either. A hard truth: if you don't feel excited about leading, perhaps there's someone else God is calling into the role of leader. Think and pray about that.

If nobody else is having fun, why do you expect them to come back? You don't have to be a stand-up comedian to lighten up the vibe of your class, but you do need to take yourself less seriously than you take the Bible truths you share.

So relax. Smile. Find the humor in what people say or do, and together seek to find joy in Jesus. It's there.

CHAPTER 8

GUIDING SENIORS THROUGH CHANGE

"For many seniors change is unwelcome," says former ministry volunteer and octogenarian Judy. "When you get older things change so fast it's hard to keep up. And a lot of the changes aren't changes you want to make."

For Judy those changes included hip replacements, the death of a husband, and needing to leave the home she'd happily occupied for 45 years—all within a few years. "I'd reverse those changes in a moment if I could," she says.

Seniors in your ministry may also be coping with stressful changes they haven't initiated and wish could be rolled back. Not everyone who quits working does so willingly. Few seniors are enthused about relying on others or dealing with declining health.

Given that change is a constant for the people you serve, knowing how to assist them in coping is a handy skill.

Here are a few pointers from Judy and others:

Realize you don't know how it feels

Even if you've been in a similar situation, you aren't aware of how the senior sitting in front of you is experiencing it. Don't assume that senior has the same resources, temperament, or degree of willingness to embrace the change.

Ask how the senior is coping and then just listen.

That's how you find out how people feel.

Loss isn't a contest

Many changes feel like loss because they are.

It's tempting to try to build rapport by mentioning what you've lost in life, too, but that's almost always a mistake because rather than build a bridge it can become a wall as the focus shifts off the senior.

"When Brian passed away a friend told me how devastated she was when her pet died," remembers Judy. "All I could think of was, 'You lost a cat and I lost the love of my life. Forgive me, but I don't understand how they equal out.'"

Be a consistent support

If you're checking in on one of your seniors by phone or in person, do so at predictable times and intervals. Once you establish a pattern it's something your senior can anticipate.

"It's hard to make new friends in independent living facilities," says Judy. "For about a month, until I found a few new friends, my sons called every day. Some days they were the only people I talked to. Those calls meant more than they'll ever know."

It's a big deal if someone feels it's a big deal

Tricia laughs when she talks about her husband and change. "Even when he was younger he resisted it," she says. "A member of our small group once pointed at him and said, 'Change Is Not My Friend' should be on his family crest."

Growing older hasn't made changes any easier for Tricia's husband.

"Now that he's pushing seventy, things that once slid by under the radar bother him. It's certainly not getting easier," she says.

Your seniors might also get prickly about changes that don't seem like a big deal to you. Changing a meeting time by half an hour or switching up the Sunday school curriculum, for instance.

Repeat after me: it's a big deal if they feel it's a big deal. Honor seniors' concerns.

Be careful about spreading *too* much sunshine

"It's not like I've forgotten that God is good and a better time is coming," says Judy. "But sometimes, like on an anniversary I won't be celebrating with Brian, I don't care. I'm feeling my loss and just need to feel it."

It's not a bad thing to gently remind seniors a time is coming when pain and loss are banished, but be sure they're ready to hear that. Sometimes it's best to sit quietly, hold a senior's hand, and bear witness to their sorrow.

Remind seniors of their resilience—and that Jesus never changes

Most have survived at least one war, a flurry of technological innovations, and the process of aging itself. They've proven themselves capable of making changes in the past and, with God's help, can do so again.

Ask questions that help seniors remember their strengths and identify their support systems.

Make Hebrews 13:8 a steady drumbeat in your ministry: Jesus is the same yesterday, today, and tomorrow. He's someone who won't change and is bedrock on which to build a life.

And when it comes to making changes at church:

Seniors are sometimes seen as an obstacle to change because, well, because sometimes they are. But it's also true that seniors are very willing to deal with change if you take four simple steps to manage how change is perceived.

• **Make sure change meets an actual need.** If it's change for change's sake, expect push back. Given how much change seniors are forced to deal with, they aren't excited about making changes because of a whim.

• **Explain why the change is needed and what will happen if it isn't made.** A children's class at a midwestern church was meeting in a cramped, crowded room while adults met in a spacious lounge area flooded with light. The older crowd was reluctant to vacate their comfortable setting until they visited the children's room and saw that there was literally no space for new kids. That's all it took for the seniors to willingly relocate.

• **Be sure seniors believe the change is possible.** Think through how you'll make a change before asking for seniors' support. Even better: ask open-minded seniors to help strategize how to successfully make the change.

• **Be sure seniors see the change as an improvement.** Present changes as "experiments." That is, ask seniors to try the change for six or eight weeks and then evaluate if it improved things. Maybe the old way was better or there's a way to modify the change so it makes an improvement. Seniors who resist wholesale change are often willing to try an experiment in good faith attempt.

CHAPTER 9

IN-REACH TO SENIORS

*Y*ou have a senior adult ministry. There are seniors in your church, some actively involved and some less so. So why aren't more of your church's seniors involved in your ministry? How can you reach out to your seniors and draw them in?

Give these approaches a try:

• **Advertise programs in places seniors will see your invitation**

Seniors still open snail mail so sending a monthly calendar of activities and contact information is usually worthwhile. The same can be said for Sunday morning bulletins, up-front screen announcements, and spoken invitations made during announcement times.

• **Create multiple "entrance ramps"**

Put a table out in the church lobby before services with information about free services available to seniors in your community. As you distribute the pamphlets provided by those agencies, capture seniors' contact information so you can invite them to events hosted for seniors.

• **Connect through emails and other technology**

However you'd reach out to the rest of your congregation, do the same thing for seniors. You can find just as many seniors on the latest platforms as you'll find seniors who don't know what those platforms are.

• **Post on your church's website and Facebook page**

Yep, Seniors still check out websites. And they still look at Facebook. (Because that's where their kids post grandkid photos, that's why.)

• **Pick up the phone**

Nothing beats a personal invitation and if you don't have time to contact the seniors on your church rolls recruit a few seniors to help you.

• **Talk about the benefits of participation**

Don't give just the facts, for example, that there's a lunch at a local restaurant on Thursday at 11:30. Take it a step further and talk about how much fun it is to connect with other adults, how satisfying it is to make new friends, about how fellowship feeds the soul and sprinkles pixie dust on the day.

• **Have satisfied seniors give testimonies**

If your ministry is enriching lives, get those stories out front and center. It's one thing for *you* to say great things about the adult Sunday school class. It's another for people in the *class* to say the same thing.

• **Keep the welcome mat rolled out**

Things change in seniors' lives. Someone who's been too busy to be part of your ministry may be in a very different spot in six months. Let seniors know they're always welcome whether they come to every meeting and event or catch just a few.

Either way, you'll be there for them.

And by all means nail shut the back door:

Younger generations aren't the only ones declaring themselves done with church. Seniors, too, are leaving in record numbers.

For many reasons it's a good idea to keep seniors actively growing in their faith. That won't happen if your church settles for the typical Sunday routine of "plop, pray, and pay."

There's got to be more. There have to be opportunities to engage and serve.

Seniors relegated to spectator status often don't stick around. They want to be contributing and, if there's no place to do that in your ministry and church, they'll find a volunteer role outside the church that works for them.

Consider hosting a senior "job" fair. Where are senior-friendly opportunities to volunteer in your ministry and other church ministries? At minimum get brief job descriptions and contact information and give the list to your seniors.

If there aren't many options for volunteering and serving, sit down with your pastor and ask why not. What could change that would include senior adults more completely?

Maybe you don't think your church has a problem with senior adult opportunities. After all, when seniors don't show up on Sunday morning it's often assumed they're simply tired. Or maybe they're with the grandkids or galivanting off on another long-weekend vacation in Vegas.

Do this: ask a representative sample of your seniors to give you honest answers to these questions:

- Why are you involved in this church?
- What keeps you here instead of going somewhere else or nowhere at all?
- If you've considered leaving, why?
- What would help you grow in your faith?
- If you could serve in some way you're not now serving, what would it be?

The answers you hear will give you a sense of how fulfilled your seniors are with your ministry and church. You'll see how your ministry might more effectively meet your seniors' needs.

CHAPTER 10

OUTREACH TO SENIORS

*A*sk the leaders of your senior adult ministry, "Is your ministry just for those inside your church or are you open to others joining you as well?"

If your mission is to help seniors know Jesus and grow in their faith, it would seem to be a no-brainer you want to reach as many seniors as possible. Churched, unchurched, other-churched—they're all likely to benefit from what you're doing.

But you may face the challenge of growing beyond your resources and ability to follow up with seniors. Training leaders, forming additional small groups, adding events to the calendar: growing means growing pains.

So plan now how to make your ministry sustainable as it grows.

Start by getting clarity about who you're going to minister to. Assuming that includes seniors who aren't already in your church, following are ways to reach out to those them.

Answer the WIIFM question

Be ready when a senior asks you this question: "What's In It For Me?"

It's a reasonable question. You're asking for the time and attention of seniors; what will they get in return? Why should they become a part of your ministry rather than join the Elks Club or volunteer at the local soup kitchen?

We can't answer that question for you, but we can tell you this: in one form or another, it's coming. When it does, be ready to share what difference your ministry is making in the lives of seniors and what needs you're meeting.

Have low barriers to entry

Seniors aren't typically excited about signing on to a once-a-week meeting even when they know you. It's an uphill climb to get seniors who don't know you to make a commitment.

Dan Johnson is the chaplain of Great Lakes Christian Home, a Michigan independent living facility. You'd think a facility with the word "Christian" in the name would be a hot-bed of long-standing Bible studies and on-going service projects.

And you'd be wrong.

"We don't do things that require long-term commitments," says Johnson. "Seniors have a sense that more of their lives are behind than ahead of them. The older they grow, the more they approach life with a day-by-day, short-term perspective."

Some of seniors' reluctance to make long-term term commitments has to do with their awareness a commitment might outlive them. But there are also health concerns, transportation issues, and the need to stay flexible to care for others. And sometimes it's that seniors just want a break.

Whatever the reason for reluctance, this hesitancy means you'll be better able to draw in a senior with a one-shot program than a 13-week Sunday school class.

So host a one-hour "How to Enjoy Retirement" seminar or a "What You Need to Know About Wills" lecture by an attorney. Rally seniors to support a good cause or show up for a game or trivia night. You'll find dozens of possible activities in chapters 11 and 12.

Which ones can you adapt to bring in seniors who can then hear about other programs in your ministry?

Be willing to not preach

This feels counter-intuitive but hear us out.

Sometimes it's better not to lead with Jesus. Give non-believers the chance to get to know you before you evangelize or share a devotion.

One congregation organized a river-bank clean-up day and made sure hiking clubs, environmental groups, and local senior service clubs knew about it. The day started with a prayer for safety, but that was the last obviously Christian element to the day other than this: seniors from the church were intentional about working alongside seniors they didn't know.

Spiritual conversations were prompted when seniors in the ministry asked their non-churched work buddies why they were motivated to clean up nature. When the question was returned, the ministry seniors talked about the beauty of God's creation.

Several friendships were sparked that made it possible to invite those new contacts to additional programs. It's not a bad first impression for community seniors to think of your senior adult ministry and church as caring, and your ministry members as friendly.

Emphasize personal invitations

By far the most effective way to grow your number of seniors is for your group members to invite friends. No clever advertising campaign or website can begin to compare with Larry asking his friend Jack to check out an activity Larry enjoys.

So if your leadership gives you the okay to grow your corner of the ministry, talk with seniors about inviting friends. If they're reluctant, ask why. What would have to change for seniors to feel comfortable inviting friends?

If you advertise, do so strategically

Advertising will likely be done by your leadership but keep an eye open for places you can spread the word at little or no cost.

- Ask seniors who are part of community service groups to mention your ministry there.
- Write a letter to the editor of your local paper suggesting one way for seniors to combat isolation is to join groups like yours.
- Get listed in the "Community Events" section of free "After 50" newspapers.
- Ask Christian schools to distribute flyers that suggest ideas for grandchild/grandparent involvement, along with information about your ministry.
- Take posters to senior centers, retirement homes, anywhere seniors congregate.
- Sympathetic secular agencies may also pass along information about entry-ramp programs once they're comfortable with you and your programs.

Keep your message simple and advertise where seniors will see the information. And remember if you're creating posters to do so in large print.

Pray, always

Ask God to bring the people who'll benefit from your ministry to you.

Greet them warmly.

CHAPTER 11

ENGAGING GO-GO'S, SLOW-GO'S, AND NO-GO'S

*S*enior adult ministries engage seniors with a wide range of activities: Sunday school classes, outings, service projects, small groups, retreats, mentoring, everything from stuffing envelopes to stuffing themselves at barbeques and potlucks.

The principal behind engagement is simple: you've got to give seniors something to do once they show up. Fall short on that and you'll see seniors disengage as quickly as they engaged in the first place.

You may or may not be in charge of selecting activities for your senior adult ministry. If you are, following is a list of 61 to consider. If you aren't, show this list to seniors you serve and see which activities they find most interesting. Pass that information on to your ministry leaders.

As noted in Chapter 5, your seniors can be sorted into three general groupings: Go-Go's who are active, may be still working, and may have family nearby. Slow-Go's are slowing down but still out and about. No-Go's can no longer come to church because they're homebound or in care facilities.

It's nearly impossible to find activities ideal for all three groups, so offer enough activities that there's something to engage everyone.

Here, in no particular order, are activities that could find a home in your ministry. Use them as sparks to fire up your thinking about how they could be tweaked to be a perfect fit for your situation.

- **Create and either mail or deliver "Glad you came" packages to church visitors.**

Include a brief summary of what's available at your church, an inexpensive New Testament, and a handwritten note with the name and phone number of a contact person.

- **Own a service ministry of your church.** Become the official Usher Team or Parking Lot Team during large church events. Pick an area that allows your seniors to both serve and get to know one another better.

CASE STUDY: DANCING DAN

One large church occasionally hosts concerts. Christian comedians or musicians come for an evening and a thousand cars have to smoothly enter and exit the parking lot.

Enter Dancing Dan and his cronies.

"You know how those guys at airports guide planes in to the jetways by waving big flashlights? That's Dan and the crew," says a church staffer who'd rather not be named. "They've got entire choreographies worked out and they're always trying to outdo each other. Nobody has more fun serving in our church than the parking lot crew."

The pastor is fairly certain that on some concert nights the best part of the show is in the parking lot. "Mix sign spinners, airplane guides, and professional cheerleads and you've got Dancing Dan and his boys. They're a hoot." Those boys are all about 70, by the way. And they're not about to give up their posts.

Asked why he doesn't want to go on record, the pastor says he'd rather not drive home some night only to find the parking lot performers guiding him the last block or two to his driveway. "I wouldn't put it past them," says the pastor.

• **Become links in the church prayer chain.** But instead of just sending text messages or phoning to alert others of the need to pray train your seniors to pray right on the spot with those they're alerting.

• **Take field trips.** Anything educational, informational, recreational, or just plain fun can qualify, but make sure there's a spiritual component.

• **Become foster grandparents.** In your congregation are there young children who have no grandparents? If that's the case, ask seniors to "adopt" those kids, to greet them on Sundays, remember their birthdays, and show up at occasional school plays or basketball games. Arrange everything through the children's parents and require seniors to have background checks.

• **Hold a quarterly game night at church.** Think Bingo, board games, card games, or even set up a few Velcro dart boards in the corner. Provide snacks and keep things moving so seniors don't get bored.

CAUTIONARY CASE STUDY: MIKE

"My daughter was part of a youth group in another church," says Mike. "Parents of youth group kids were invited in for snacks and a Skip-Bo night. I thought it would be great to meet other people raising teenagers."

Mike had never heard of Skip-Bo. He went into the evening not knowing how to play and still doesn't know.

"There were probably 50 of us seated at card tables. I was with a few very competitive players who wouldn't stop to explain the rules because it was a timed event."

Mike quickly made a series of blunders that angered his partner. There was no time to have a conversation and when the whistle blew the winning pair of players was off to play with other winning pairs. Mike was shuttled over to play with other "Losers."

"I finally just left," says Mike. "No more church game nights for me. It only takes a few people more intent on winning than enjoying fellowship to ruin the whole evening."

The caution: If you host a game night for your seniors, be very, very clear winning is less important than enjoying one another. Between games pause to toss out a discussion question or request seniors to share memories of games they played as hildren.

• **Organize seniors helping seniors Saturdays.** Send retired Go-Go plumber Bob to tighten up dripping faucets in the homes of seniors who can't do this themselves. What other skills do your seniors have that could be put to use helping others at no cost?

• **Host an intergenerational meal.** Recruit youth group members to share a meal with seniors some evening. Provide the food and set discussion cards at each table. Cards might include: "What was your favorite treat when you were a child?," or "If there's a meaning to your name, explain what it is.," or "What's the worst pet name you've heard? The best? If someone gave you a boa constrictor as a pet, what would you name it?"

You get the idea.

• **Create a way homebound seniors can take part in Sunday school and worship services.** Having streaming services available on the church website isn't helpful if seniors either don't have technology or can't figure out how to use it. See how many of those problems you can solve.

• **Instant Orchestra.** Have everyone dust off their instruments and bring them in for a time of making music. Recruit a patient conductor and keep the sheet music simple.

• **Hymn Sings.** Rather than letting seniors stew about how the worship team has cut their favorite songs from the set list, rustle up a piano player and let seniors who want to sing all 43 verses of "Just As I Am" have at it.

• **Volunteer in an after-school program.** If your church is near an elementary school, ask the principal what it would take to volunteer in the school's program.

CASE STUDY: CINDY

Cindy is the Christian Education director in a small Ohio town. Her church has a gymnasium that's used only occasionally on weekday afternoons. An elementary school is directly across a side street. "I saw that as an opportunity," says Cindy.

She did a bit of research and realized she could open up the gym as an after-school safe space, but to do so required lots of adult supervision. The solution: seniors.

"Some of the older adults supervise games, some help with homework, some serve snacks," says Cindy. "Some just sit and talk with lonely kids."

Some days there are more than a hundred children in the gym in the hours between school dismissal and when parents get off work. These are kids who would have been home alone playing video games and instead they're hanging out with us making friends."

Cindy keeps things simple, calling what happens a drop-in open-gym rather than an after-school program, which means she doesn't have to deal with tons of regulations.

But she does need to have ample volunteers. "Seniors to the rescue," she smiles.

• **Advocate for Seniors—in a *nice* way.** Don't storm city hall but check with the library about how many large print books are shelved. Inquire of city government how seniors who can't access websites and aren't able to hear on the phone can easily pay their utility bills. Gently raise awareness in local businesses of the challenges faced by their elderly customers.

- **Host a scrapbooking class.** Tell seniors now is the time to organize papers and mementos that document their lives. Help seniors tell their stories and ask to hear those stories yourself.

- **Organize fast food friends.** Drive-through sack lunches aren't always the healthiest, but for No-Go's starving for fellowship that won't matter. Arrange for Go-Go's and Slow-Go's to visit No-Go's every few weeks to have lunch in the latter's homes. A quick phone call to find out what the No-Go would like from Burger Buddy lets the visitor show up with a restaurant meal the No-Go can no longer get for herself, plus whatever the visitor is eating.

- **Mentoring gives meaning.** Invite older adults to become short-term mentors for children, youth, and even other adults. A few places to plug in mentors: helping children with Confirmation activities, getting new church members established by introducing them to programs and people, and being study buddies to kids who are struggling with schoolwork.

- **Provide pet walking.** Slow-Go's and No-Go's can benefit mightily from having a dog or cat around but mobility issues may make playing with or exercising those pets a challenge. Organize stopping by regularly to provide a pet play and exercise service. If possible, have the pet owners join you on a brief walk or "fetch" session. Exercise is good for the elderly, too.

- **Create a newsletter for your older adults.** Share health tips, talk about upcoming events, interview different seniors and share their backstories. One assisted living facility launched a newsletter and in searching for stories quickly discovered among the residents were the former mayor, a sailor who'd served in a submarine, and a retired Rockette!

- **Provide passages.** An older adult is leaving a home of 50 years to move into a one-bedroom assisted living apartment. Help with the transition by walking through the rooms of the empty house and listening to stories about what happened there. Pray with the transitioning senior. Read the account of Abram trusting God as he stepped into the unknown. Once the senior is settled into the new location, meet there to pray God's blessing on the new home.

• **Celebrate each Senior Year.** Annually, create a printed "Senior Yearbook" that includes photos of ministry events in the past year. Encourage seniors to sign one another's books.

• **Do daily check-ins.** Every day make a call to the No-Go's to make sure they're all right. No pick-up? Try again in several hours. Still nothing? Have arranged with No-Go's who they want notified who can then physically check on unresponsive No-Go's.

• **Support your church staff.** Get to know these servants and occasionally surprise them with appropriate, encouraging gifts. And no "everyone gets the same coffee mug" gifts; instead, buy a travel magazine subscription for that staffer who loves travel, a new wood file for the staff member who relaxes with wood carving. Gifts shouldn't be expensive—they're given to communicate "we see you, like you, and love you." Letters of encouragement are always welcome, too.

• **Send cards and letters.** Seniors still remember how to write them so tap seniors to send anniversary, birthday, and "thinking of you" cards to members of the congregation.

• **Organize Operation Christmas Child or another church-wide project for the congregation.** Several seasonal efforts could bring together all your seniors to serve together. A list of possible projects is in Chapter 12.

• **Start and maintain a community garden.** Be sure extra vegetables make their way to food banks or families in need. Look to connect with participants and teach them how to do their own gardens in lawns or flowerpots.

And here's a quick list of additional service projects to run by your seniors:

- Collect gently used clothing and donate it to a homeless shelter.

- Organize a blood drive for the church or community.
- Do light janitorial duty following services.
- Set up rooms for weddings, dinners, special events.
- Collect items for military care packages sent to service personnel.
- Decorate the church building for holidays.
- Organize and staff a church "Trunk or Treat" for Halloween.
- Do a day of yard work at the home of a senior who's house-bound.
- Be volunteer readers/storytellers at the Library
- Create or curate art exhibits in the lobby of your church building.
- Host an AAA meeting in your church building.
- Invite an ESL teacher to meet with students in your facility.
- Meet to fold church bulletins, staple sermon note pages, or other easy-to-chat-while-doing tasks.
- Teach a basic sign language class and provide interpreters for church meetings.
- Provide meals to new moms and newly discharged patients.
- Take packaged goodies to police stations and fire departments for their break rooms.
- Create birthday party boxes for use at homeless shelters.
- Do a diaper drive for a local pregnancy center.
- Fill backpacks with school supplies for children in low-income schools.
- Leave new coloring books and boxes of crayons in hospital ER lounges.

- Help a refugee family navigate registering kids for school and filling out paperwork.
- Cheer like crazy at a Special Olympics event.
- Do a seniors car wash—but no swimsuits. We don't want to scare the children!
- Host a high tea for young children to attend with their parents.
- Organize a gingerbread house building event.
- Adopt a local elementary school and, just before school opens for the year, give a day to cleaning classrooms.
- Invite patient teenagers in to help seniors figure out their smart phones.
- If you have a capable instructor, host a line-dancing class.
- Invite a local college's music department to have a few students perform for you.
- Go to a play with other seniors.
- Karaoke!
- Clear the parking lot and ask a local classic car club to stop by.
- Host a senior trivia night.
- Carpool to a local farmer's market and talk about how peppers used to taste better.
- Initiate pet therapy—invite seniors to enjoy a fresh litter of puppies on the church lawn.
- Did we mention Karaoke? (That was a bad idea. Forget that one.)

CHAPTER 12

13 SENIOR-SIZED SERVICE PROJECTS

Service projects come in two flavors: those within your church body and those that take your seniors out into the community. Both can be powerful in prompting spiritual growth in your seniors.

Consider hosting a "job fair" where various ministry roles within your church are explained to your seniors. Have representatives come from various ministries including Ushers, Greeters, Information Table personnel, Children's Ministry, Hospitality, Congregational Care, Security, Parking, Coffee Table, Office, and Janitorial. Who else could explain volunteer roles? Invite them, too.

When it comes to community projects, decide if you want to invent the wheel or roll with an existing program. The easiest option is to connect with Habitat for Humanity, the Community Soup Kitchen, or another Christ-focused ministry that's well organized and serving others. But don't be afraid of partnering with a secular agency as well, so long as you determine it's not actually hostile to Christ or the Church. You can add spiritual elements to the experience through a group-huddle prayer before starting to serve and debriefing the experience through the lens of your faith following the experience.

Here's a baker's dozen of service ideas to explore:

1. Host a church-wide picnic or potluck after worship services. Have group games, but only games your seniors remember playing when they were children.

2. Create and staff a Seniors Exercise and Fitness Class. Invite local health clubs to participate; they'll love the exposure, provide expertise, and likely offer discounted memberships to seniors who complete the course.

3. Deliver flowers to No-Go Seniors. Recipients can be members of your congregation or just residents in a nearby facility. Check with the facility to find out what regulations apply and when would be best to provide this service. Consider making deliveries not around holidays; there can be an outpouring of thoughtful gifts at holidays and then . . . nothing.

4. Start a food or clothing pantry. Too complicated? How about adopting a day or two each month to provide staffing at existing pantries?

5. Safety inspector Saturday. Check with the local fire department to find out where to get a stack of inexpensive smoke detectors. Arrange to visit seniors' homes to make sure there are sufficient detectors in place. Replace any dead batteries in existing detectors and, if there aren't enough detectors, install a few.

6. What retirement? Tap your seniors who have teaching backgrounds to see if they'd be interested in leading brief enrichment programs in their areas of expertise. But be aware that some educators, once they've hung up their classroom spurs, aren't eager to get back in the saddle.

CASE STUDY: TERRY

Terry was an effective elementary and special education teacher for decades. He was even named Teacher of the Year by his district a time or two. After retiring he subbed to cover a few classes, mentored new teachers, and shared his insights at professional meetings.

But he's now pulled the plug on even those activities.

"I'm done with kids and parents," he says. "Fifty years was enough."

So ask Terry to teach Sunday school and you'll get a hard "no." He may be qualified, but he's not interested. What he really likes to do—what he's first in line for after every snowstorm in his Wisconsin town—is to fire up a snowblower.

"We call it the Snowblower Brigade," Terry says of a group of church men who four-wheel drive it to the church to clear sidewalks and get the parking lot passable. "We work until it's done and then meet at a coffee shop to relax and solve the world's problems."

He's serving, but not as an educator. And for the first time in his life he looks forward to winter storm warnings.

7. Cover church office phones. If there's not much action in the office but your church would still like to be able to have a live person answer the phone during office hours, recruit a set of seniors to take turns making that happen between nine and noon daily. Bonus: Most phone systems have a way to forward calls during designated times so the seniors can answer from home. Downside: there's very little socializing.

8. Staff a nursing home Sunday school. Bring a critical mass of seniors (four or five will do) and do a repeat of your Sunday school in the community room of a local nursing home. Invite residents to attend. Caution: keep the focus on Scripture, not doctrine because you'll have participants from all sorts of backgrounds.

9. Hold a community Easter Egg Hunt. A church plant got permission to do an Easter Egg Hunt on the grounds of the school they were renting for services. The church advertised the free event through the school and community outlets. On the day of the event, a hired school janitor opened up the building for access to restrooms and ran electric cords to power up the outdoor sound system. Various areas of the lawn were roped off for different ages of egg hunters, bouncy castles were brought in, popcorn and Icee machines were fired up, and a prop-filled "Funny Foto" booth was set up. Parents registered to participate which made sending out already prepared "thanks for coming!" follow-ups the next day easy. Multiple families returned to visit the church.

10. Adopt a missionary family. Research the ages and interests of family members so you can send appropriate Christmas and birthday gifts as well as occasional care packages. Tanya was a missionary kid in southern Italy and sixty years later still recalls fondly the packages she received from a church in Springfield, Ohio, all throughout her childhood. "Though I always wondered why they shipped us cans of Chef Boyardee spaghetti when we were in Italy," she says.

11. Adopt a meals-on wheels route. To make sure this has some relational value within your group, send out drivers in twos or threes. Extra points if they're choir members and can sing a cheery song when they make deliveries. Extra, *extra* points if they can pull off a barbershop quartet number.

12. Tape a dozen ten-dollar bills to your pastor's door, preferably when the pastor is home. Also tape a note: "We TP'd your house, but not the way the youth group would have done it. You're a blessing!" Ring the doorbell and run for the get-away car. Brings back memories, doesn't it?

13. Host a block party for the streets adjacent to your church property. Refreshments, a bounce castle, lawn games. Make it a "get to know you" event and find out how you're perceived as a neighbor. Deliver invitations to homes well in advance and ask for an RSVP so you can right-size the homemade snacks.

And here's a bonus service idea:

Go Christmas caroling—in July. Explain the cheer and message of Christmas matters all year long. Visit homes or set up on a street corner or a busy pedestrian area. Invite passers-by to join you for a song or two. If you've got a Santa look-alike feel free to pass out small gifts to kids who come by.

CHAPTER 13

SHORT-TERM MISSION OPPORTUNITIES

Q: What's the difference between a Short-Term Mission and a service project?
A: Short term missions usually require packing a suitcase.

Short-term missions typically involve a long weekend or full week of service. It may be staffing a VBS in an inner-city park, building a new dorm for a Hattian orphanage, or holding a pop-up medical clinic in Ethiopia. But mission trips don't always require travel. That park could be just a few miles from your church, the orphanage that needs help across town, and the medical clinic held after hours at a local medical office.

What makes short-term missions unique is they're typically cross-cultural. And expensive. And challenging to pull off on your own, especially if you're a volunteer in your ministry. A mission trip needs leadership to be on board.

And there's this: where do you go to find a mission trip that's both spiritually based and appropriate for seniors?

The same place you'll find anything else: online.

ShortTermMissions.com is a one-stop shop to review 979 different trips provided by 65 organizations. But don't hold us to those numbers—they're always shifting as organizations decide what trips to offer or whether they'll offer trips at all. Some trips are geared for students but will accept seniors and others won't. Some trips as more or less physically demanding than others. It's impossible to provide an exhaustive list of options in print; you'll have to get online to do some homework.

But before you ask your leaders about a trip, do this:

Pray

Is a short-term mission something Jesus has in mind for your seniors? If so, what kind of trip will both serve others and help your seniors to grow in their faith?

Check with denominational headquarters, if you have one

Are there trips already organized by your denomination that will meet your needs? If so, it will be easy to get your questions answered and you'll know what to expect theologically.

Ask around

Who do you know who's gone on a short-term mission? What was it like? How did it impact that person's life? Would they go again? What would they change about the experience?

Get referrals

Every mission organization paints its offerings as ideal for your seniors, but that's not always the case. Call potential mission providers and get referrals. Then Google unique language from the organization's mission names and see if you can find blogs or Facebook references you can read. They'll be unfiltered.

Consider having a *Secondhand* Mission Trip

That is, if your church's youth group is heading overseas to do mission work, how can you help them get there? Can you provide moral support? Financial support? How about asking your seniors to come up with a list of do-able jobs around their homes they're willing to pay a teenager to do?

Seniors serving your church's senior-high students is a wonderful thing, too.

CHAPTER 14

SCRIPTURES THAT SPEAK
TO THE NEEDS OF SENIORS

The Bible doesn't address every issue that might pop up in a senior's life. There's no passage that directly mentions losing one's driver's license, for instance. But many passages declare truths that apply to general needs and situations.

Get familiar with those that follow. You'll want to point to them when seniors need reminders they're not alone and God is with them.

Accepting Change

"Therefore I tell you, do not worry about your life, what you will eat or drink; or about your body, what you will wear. Is not life more than food, and the body more than clothes?" (Matthew 6:25)

And we know that in all things God works for the good of those who love him, who have been called according to his purpose. (Romans 8:28)

Jesus Christ is the same yesterday and today and forever. (Hebrews 13:8)

Comfort

The LORD is a refuge for the oppressed, a stronghold in times of trouble. (Psalm 9:9)

Cast your cares on the Lord and he will sustain you; he will never let the righteous be shaken. (Psalm 55:22)

He heals the brokenhearted and binds up their wounds. (Psalm 147:3)

"Come to me, all you who are weary and burdened, and I will give you rest." (Matthew 11:28)

Confidence

...being confident of this, that he who began a good work in you will carry it on to completion until the day of Christ Jesus. (Philippians 1:6)

I can do all this through him who gives me strength. (Philippians 4:13)

Contentment

I know what it is to be in need, and I know what it is to have plenty. I have learned the secret of being content in any and every situation, whether well fed or hungry, whether living in plenty or in want. I can do all this through him who gives me strength. (Philippians 4:11-12)

But godliness with contentment is great gain. (1 Timothy 6:6)

Keep your lives free from the love of money and be content with what you have, because God has said, "Never will I leave you; never will I forsake you." (Hebrews 13:5)

Death

Now if we died with Christ, we believe that we will also live with him. For we know that since Christ was raised from the dead, he cannot die again; death no longer has mastery over him. (Romans 6:8-9)

For the wages of sin is death, but the gift of God is eternal life in Christ Jesus our Lord. (Romans 6:23)

"Where, O death, is your victory? Where, O death, is your sting?" (Romans 15:55)

Depression

God is our refuge and strength, an ever-present help in trouble. Therefore we will not fear, though the earth give way and the mountains fall into the heart of the sea... (Psalm 46:1-2)

Dear friends, do not be surprised at the fiery ordeal that has come on you to test you, as though something strange were happening to you. But rejoice inasmuch as you participate in the sufferings of Christ, so that you may be overjoyed when his glory is revealed. (1 Peter 4:12-13)

We are hard pressed on every side, but not crushed; perplexed, but not in despair; persecuted, but not abandoned; struck down, but not destroyed. (2 Corinthians 4:8-9)

Encouragement

Wait for the LORD; be strong and take heart and wait for the LORD. (Psalm 27:14)

"And surely I am with you always, to the very end of the age." (Matthew 28:20b)

Okay to copy this page for personal use

When I said, "My foot is slipping," your unfailing love, Lord, supported me. When anxiety was great within me, your consolation brought me joy. (Psalm 94:18-19)

So we say with confidence, "The Lord is my helper; I will not be afraid. What can mere mortals do to me? (Hebrews 13:6)

Fear

The Lord is my light and my salvation—whom shall I fear? The Lord is the stronghold of my life—of whom shall I be afraid? (Psalm 27:1)

There is no fear in love. But perfect love drives out fear, because fear has to do with punishment. The one who fears is not made perfect in love. (1 John 4:18)

Even though I walk through the darkest valley, I will fear no evil, for you are with me; your rod and your staff, they comfort me. (Psalm 23:4)

Grief

The LORD is close to the brokenhearted and saves those who are crushed in spirit. (Psalm 34:18)

Blessed are those who mourn, for they will be comforted. (Matthew 5:4)

Godly sorrow brings repentance that leads to salvation and leaves no regret, but worldly sorrow brings death. (2 Corinthians 7:10)

Happiness

I keep my eyes always on the Lord. With him at my right hand, I will not be shaken. Therefore my heart is glad and my tongue rejoices; my body also will rest secure... (Psalm 16:8-9)

Rejoice in the Lord always. I will say it again: Rejoice! (Philippians 4:4)

Health

For physical training is of some value, but godliness has value for all things, holding promise for both the present life and the life to come. This is a trustworthy saying that deserves full acceptance. (1 Timothy 4:8-9)

Our days may come to seventy years, or eighty, if our strength endures; yet the best of them are but trouble and sorrow, for they quickly pass, and we fly away. (Psalm 90:10)

A cheerful heart is good medicine, but a crushed spirit dries up the bones. (Proverbs 17:22)

Hope

Be strong and take heart, all you who hope in the LORD. (Psalm 31:24)

Be joyful in hope, patient in affliction, faithful in prayer. (Romans 12:12)

May the God of hope fill you with all joy and peace as you trust in him, so that you may overflow with hope by the power of the Holy Spirit. (Romans 15:13)

What no eye has seen, what no ear has heard, and what no human mind has conceived"—the things God has prepared for those who love him... (1 Corinthians 2:9)

Loneliness

I will not leave you as orphans; I will come to you. (John 14:18)

Turn to me and be gracious to me, for I am lonely and afflicted. (Psalm 25:16)

Okay to copy this page for personal use

Money

Honor the Lord with your wealth, with the firstfruits of all your crops... (Proverbs 3:9)

So do not worry, saying, 'What shall we eat?' or 'What shall we drink?' or 'What shall we wear?' For the pagans run after all these things, and your heavenly Father knows that you need them. But seek first his kingdom and his righteousness, and all these things will be given to you as well. (Matthew 6:31-33)

And my God will meet all your needs according to the riches of his glory in Christ Jesus. (Philippians 4:19)

Peace

"I have told you these things, so that in me you may have peace. In this world you will have trouble. But take heart! I have overcome the world." (John 16:33)

Now may the Lord of peace himself give you peace at all times and in every way. The Lord be with all of you. (2 Thessalonians 3:16)

You will keep in perfect peace those whose minds are steadfast, because they trust in you. (Isaiah 26:3)

Peace I leave with you; my peace I give you. I do not give to you as the world gives. Do not let your hearts be troubled and do not be afraid. (John 14:27)

Purpose

Many are the plans in a person's heart, but it is the LORD's purpose that prevails. (Proverbs 19:21)

Okay to copy this page for personal use

He has shown you, O mortal, what is good. And what does the LORD require of you? To act justly and to love mercy and to walk humbly with your God. (Micah 6:8)

Therefore go and make disciples of all nations, baptizing them in the name of the Father and of the Son and of the Holy Spirit, and teaching them to obey everything I have commanded you. And surely I am with you always, to the very end of the age." (Matthew 28:19-20)

Seeking God

Trust in the LORD with all your heart and lean not on your own understanding… (Proverbs 3:5)

Jesus answered, "I am the way and the truth and the life. No one comes to the Father except through me. (John 14:6)

Whoever finds their life will lose it, and whoever loses their life for my sake will find it. (Matthew 10:39)

Self-Image

I praise you because I am fearfully and wonderfully made; your works are wonderful, I know that full well. (Psalm 139:14)

For we are God's handiwork, created in Christ Jesus to do good works, which God prepared in advance for us to do. (Ephesians 2:10)

Am I now trying to win the approval of human beings, or of God? Or am I trying to please people? If I were still trying to please people, I would not be a servant of Christ. (Galatians 1:10)

Stress

Do not be anxious about anything, but in every situation, by prayer and petition, with thanksgiving, present your requests to God.
(Philippians 4:6)

"Come to me, all you who are weary and burdened, and I will give you rest. Take my yoke upon you and learn from me, for I am gentle and humble in heart, and you will find rest for your souls. For my yoke is easy and my burden is light." (Matthew 11:28-30)

Suffering

I consider that our present sufferings are not worth comparing with the glory that will be revealed in us. (Romans 8:18)

And the God of all grace, who called you to his eternal glory in Christ, after you have suffered a little while, will himself restore you and make you strong, firm and steadfast. (I Peter 5:10)

Consider it pure joy, my brothers and sisters, whenever you face trials of many kinds, because you know that the testing of your faith produces perseverance. Let perseverance finish its work so that you may be mature and complete, not lacking anything. (James 1:2-4)

Worry and Trust

Those who know your name trust in you, for you, LORD, have never forsaken those who seek you. (Psalm 9:10)

The LORD is my strength and my shield; my heart trusts in him, and he helps me. My heart leaps for joy, and with my song I praise him.
(Psalm 28:7)

Okay to copy this page for personal use

HELPING SENIORS DEAL WITH LONELINESS AND GRIEF

*Y*our ministry is perfectly positioned to help seniors cope with both loneliness and grief. If a doctor were to write a prescription to treat seniors' loneliness and grief, would your ministry's name would be scrawled on the prescription pad?

Loneliness

Seniors are especially susceptible to loneliness in part because (at least in the U.S.) 27% of adults ages 60 and older live alone.[5] For those who live alone there's limited opportunity for meaningful social interaction and less chance of finding a sense of purpose in serving others.

But loneliness isn't just about being alone. It's the feeling of isolation that comes when a senior—or anyone else—isn't experiencing the relationships that person desires. Seniors can live alone and completely at ease or live with a spouse and feel desperately lonely. It's all about relationships and expectations.

Whatever someone's living situation, effective ways to cope with loneliness include exactly what your senior adult ministry can offer:

---

5   https://www.pewresearch.org/fact-tank/2020/03/10/older-people-are-more-likely-to-live-alone-in-the-u-s-than-elsewhere-in-the-world

- Connection with friends and the means by which to make new friends.
- Meaningful volunteer opportunities that enhance friendships and give purpose.
- Social engagement with a variety of individuals.
- The chance to be outside in nature while traveling to or participating in activities.

Equally important is reminding seniors that God is with them. Share with lonely seniors the passages about loneliness you'll find in Chapter 14.

Loneliness is no small thing. The Centers for Disease Control and Prevention warns that social isolation is associated with about a 50% increased risk of dementia and other serious medical conditions such as stroke and heart disease.[6]

Look and listen for signs of loneliness in your seniors. If you see it, step up to see how your ministry might better meet their relational needs.

Unless you're a mental health professional, the help your ministry provides may fall far short of what your senior needs. Loneliness and grief are often symptomatic of a deeper debilitating depression. It's easy to find yourself into deeper waters than you can navigate so pause now and identify mental health resources to which you can make referrals.

Mindful that seniors often have limited incomes, collect contact information not just of Christian counselors, but also community agencies that offer income-adjusted rates for counseling.

Got those in hand? Great. Let's take a look at how you and your senior adult ministry can address the needs of those who are experiencing grief.

---

6   https://www.cdc.gov/aging/publications/features/lonely-older-adults.html

Grief

It's not uncommon for seniors to grieve. Our later years often hold the loss of friends, spouses, careers, and stability. Feelings of insignificance can overwhelm seniors as they find themselves less energetic and productive. Seniors in your ministry may have experienced multiple deep losses within just a few years.

Your ministry can provide a place of comfort to those who grieve. Some practical ways to do so are:

- Acknowledging losses and honoring seniors' pain.
- Giving those who grieve a caring, listening ear.
- Being patient (not insisting that grieving people "get over it" on your timeline).
- Recognizing that grief isn't the enemy; hopelessness is.
- Offering (but not insisting on) touch in the form of appropriate hugs.
- Providing a non-judgmental community where it's safe to cry, to wail, to grieve, to heal.
- Reminding grieving seniors of the reality of God's love.

Loneliness and grief are both painful and debilitating. These emotions sap your seniors of joy and leave them wondering what's wrong with their faith. God can use your loving, listening, encouraging intervention to surface the pain and help it begin healing.

CHAPTER 16

BECOMING A LISTENING PLACE

*A*s a volunteer in your senior adult ministry you're perfectly positioned to help turn your ministry into a place where seniors feel seen, heard, and valued. You'll do that by listening well and modeling how to listen.

But here's some bad news: most people are awful listeners. It's to be expected. Few people take a listening class. Fewer still work to improve their listening skills because we generally assume if we're hear what others say we're listening, but hearing and listening aren't the same.

Listening well makes your ministry magnetic. Seniors are keen to go places they don't feel invisible, including your programs.

So let's fine-tune the listening in your ministry—starting with you.

What sort of listener are you?

Dr. Phillip Hunsaker, a Management Professor at the University of San Diego, and Dr. Tony Alessandra, an author and speaker, suggest that there are four general categories of listeners. Here's a quick description of each type.

• Non-Listeners don't put any effort into listening

They pretend to listen and then quickly interrupt, preferring to steer the conversation and do most of the talking. They're like overbearing hosts of radio talk shows, maintaining full control of the conversation from first to last. When you're trapped in a discussion with them you wish they'd cut to a commercial so you could escape.

• **Marginal Listeners listen—but only superficially**

Mentally they're leaping ahead, figuring out what their responses will be. They're also easily distracted by what's happening in the environment—background noise, an incoming text message, even their own thoughts.

These listeners doesn't pick up on cues a senior wants to talk about something specific. Often, Marginal Listeners miss the point completely.

Here's something dangerous about these listeners: they often *appear* to be listening but that's just a mask they've pulled on. Their thoughts are elsewhere. They've learned social etiquette but not compassion.

• **Evaluative Listeners catch words but miss meaning**

These listeners try—they really do. But they register only the words spoken, disregarding tone, body language, and facial expressions. They catch facts, but miss context, nail the message, but not the meaning.

They can easily repeat what's been said so they're confident they've listened well. Yet people who converse with these listeners often walk away feeling misunderstood or even judged.

In any conversation there are multiple channels of information coming at you. One consists of the words spoken. And those words are important. They're the speaker's best efforts to describe a situation or feeling. What's said, and left unsaid, tell you a lot. Good listeners tune into *how* those words are delivered. They take note of the emotions that accompany a speaker's words. But considering only words, however, and ignoring emotion means you miss most of the information being shared with you. A senior who says, "I suppose I'll be alone at Thanksgiving" with a sigh is sending one message. If that senior says those words while giving you a fist bump and doing a victory dance, that's a senior who's delighted she won't be stuck making a dozen pies like she's done for the last 40 years.

• **Active listeners listen deeply, focusing on understanding the speaker's point of view**

This sort of listening requires deep concentration and attention.

Active listeners pay attention to all the channels of information available in a conversation: words, feelings, and thoughts. They set aside their own thoughts and feelings to give complete attention to the speaker. They notice if a speaker's words and emotions don't seem to match, and those disconnects are worth exploring.

This sort of listener sends verbal and nonverbal signals to speakers to let them know they're being heard and understood. Not just occasional nods but also summaries of what's been said so the speaker can either confirm or clarify.

Active listeners withhold judgement; they don't pounce on inconsistencies. The best volunteers in senior adult ministry—in any ministry—are either active listeners or on their way to becoming active listeners.

So, where do you fit on the list of listeners?

If you truly want to know where you land on the list, ask several people who know you well to rate you. But only ask if you're ready to hear their answers. If they think you've got room for improvement, don't be discouraged. We *all* have room to improve.

Listening is a skill so practice improves your abilities. Think of the following tips as training exercises to strengthen your listening muscles. They'll help you listen more carefully, understand more fully, and connect more thoroughly with the seniors you serve.

• **Stream an emotional movie**

Look for a film that's long on conversations and short on car chases. Pause the movie after scenes in which actors are in intense conversations and compare notes with another viewer: What were the actors feeling? How would you paraphrase what they were saying if you were checking with them for meaning? (And, yes, "chick flicks" are the G- to genre for this exercise. If you're a guy, deal with it.)

• **Watch a movie with the sound off**

This helps you sharpen your ability to pick up on visual clues and identify emotions. Sit with another volunteer for this one and call out emotions as you see them play out on the faces of actors. Do you and your partner agree on what you're seeing?

• **Discuss emotional topics with a partner**

You'll be practicing techniques of active listening. Talk about emotional topics, not fact-based ones, about the death of a childhood pet rather than the state of the economy.

• **Relax**

When a senior is anxious, angry, or otherwise emotional, it will be helpful for you to acknowledge that emotion without diving into the deep end of the same emotion. Active listeners appropriately mirror emotions but don't get swept away by the emotion itself.

When conversations heat up maintain your cool by taking a few deep breaths and letting tension drain from your body straight through the soles of your feet into the floor. Respond, don't react.

• **Pray as you listen**

That whole "pray without ceasing" thing has full force during emotional conversations. Invite Jesus to sharpen your skills and intuition, to give you the courage to speak the truth in love and listen to others like Jesus listens to you.

• Park your agenda out by the curb

"That's something I literally do at times," says Susan, a pastor who happens to be a senior herself. "I jot on a pad of paper what concerns are in the way of my being present. And I leave that list on the car seat. Those worries will be right there when I return—I won't accidentally forget them."

Susan knows she can't actively listen if her mind drifts back to her own issues while she's listening to others. Take a cue from Susan and keep a pad of paper in your car, pocket, or purse. And use it.

• Minimize distractions

Active listeners pull a chair up close to the person they're listening to, for several reasons.

First, it's easier to hear and be heard when you're not shouting across the room. You're also narrowing your focus to just the senior with whom you're speaking. You won't be distracted by people passing by or other conversations. And then there's this: seniors are sometimes either visually impaired, hard of hearing, or both.

"My mother is 91 and has glaucoma and hearing loss," says Greg. "She's also just vain enough that rather than let you know she can't quite see or hear you she nods along like she's taking in everything. She isn't."

Moving close to someone like Greg's mother is the only way you'll be able to connect with her.

• Listen with your body, too

One important way to communicate you're listening is to *look* like you're listening. Maintain frequent eye contact but not to the point you appear to be hypnotizing the senior you're listening to.

Avoid checking your watch or a clock on the wall. Silence your phone and tuck it away. If you're seated, keep an open, inviting posture. No crossed arms or legs. And if you're a fidgeter, do your best to stay still.

• Be mindful of facial expressions

A yawn signals you're bored or too tired to pay attention. A frown sends the message you disapprove of what you're hearing. An eye roll in almost any conversation is deadly.

Do this: Wear a pleasant smile as you begin the conversation and then, when you've discerned how the senior is feeling, lightly mirror that emotion in your countenance.

Your job as a listener isn't to cheer up a depressed senior by pulling out a joke or anecdote about something funny that happened to you. Seldom is it a good idea to switch on your inner stand-up comic. Far better to take the emotional temperature of the room and reflect it back.

• Stay engaged mentally

In school you learned to appear to be listening as a teacher droned on. Why? Because woe to any student who got caught mentally napping.

Don't dust off that skill to use with your seniors, even if they're slow to get to the point.

One way to not shift into Marginal Listener Mode is to picture what the senior is describing. Whether it's a literal story or a concept you can stay engaged by creating a mental picture of what's being described.

That keeps you present and in the moment, which makes your listening more effective.

• Keep these phrases handy

They may feel awkward at first, but these five phrases help you reflect back what a senior is telling you. Occasionally summarizing what you're hearing in a conversation helps you keep stories straight, especially if they're complex or muddled.

The following is your cheat sheet. Start with one of these phrases and then summarize:

"I'm wondering if I have this straight. Are you saying …?"

"So I hear you saying …"

"I'm curious. Are you saying …?"

"Am I right that you're feeling …?"

"It sounds like …"

Any phrase that tentatively mirrors what you think you're hearing gives a senior the chance to confirm, clarify, or correct. Any of those move the conversation forward.

• Ask follow-up questions

Follow-up questions build on something the senior has already said. For example, "You mentioned your wife's death shook your faith in God. I'm wondering if you'd talk more about that. What has that shake-up looked like?"

Asking follow-up questions practically shouts that you're listening and invites ever-greater depths of sharing.

• Be okay with silence

Sometimes words (however well motivated) are unwanted noise. Be okay if the senior you're with prefers you sit quietly with her or silently pray with her. If the senior leads you toward a time of silence, follow. It's your presence that's most important anyway.

• If your own emotions get in the way, say so—and move on

If the senior with you is wishing for death and you believe life is precious, that's going to impact you. It did Mark, anyway.

"I've had seniors ask me to kill them," he says. "They're in pain, facing imminent death, and they just want it all to end. One man who was homebound and bed-ridden told me he'd waited too long to shoot himself, but he told me where he kept his gun. He wanted me to pull the trigger."

Mark wasn't about to do it and said so. "I was rattled," he admits. "I told the man I couldn't kill him, but I'd pray that he'd experience peace and relief. And I reminded him that when he died he'd find both in heaven. It was a tough visit."

Mark set boundaries and was also transparent about his discomfort. Being honest with the senior let mark then move past the request to safer ground.

• **Explore feelings carefully**

If you detect an emotion, gingerly name it and see if the senior owns it. You might say, "When you talk about your grown kids I think I hear disappointment in your voice. Do I have that right?"

If the senior agrees, take that as an invitation to move the conversation deeper. You might follow up with, "I'm wondering if you can tell me more. How do you deal with that disappointment?"

Notice you've kept the conversation on the senior, not taken a shot at his kids.

When you explore emotions and seniors dive deep, it's not unusual to hear they've never talked about the topic before, that it's a weight they've carried alone. But now they feel heard. And seen. And no longer alone.

• **Don't interrupt—even to help**

As you're listening you may hit spots in the conversation where the senior takes a long pause or even sounds confused, where sentences taper off unfinished, where the senior struggles to find the right word.

Just wait patiently. Don't interrupt. You're seeing someone sort through his thoughts and feelings in real time—and that *takes* time.

Rushing in to finish a senior's sentence may strike you as helpful but you may be leading the conversation from where it might have gone. And it's not exactly respectful.

If you do feel compelled to interrupt, do so tentatively: "I think I hear you saying you're scared about moving to the facility—am I reading that right?"

• **Remember acceptance isn't endorsement**

Seniors (like all adults) are opinionated. And their opinions about politics, the church, God, and other people may not align with yours. Unless a senior's beliefs interfere with his ability to connect with God's comfort and grace, there's not much value in getting into a debate or Bible study. But if something's flat out wrong and could lead to alienation from God, say what you have to say.

• **Save your solutions**

When seniors share their challenges you might want to save the day with a quick solution. Resist the temptation. Instead, listen well and help the senior discover his or her *own* solution, one far likelier to be implemented than anything you recommend. Plus, lots of problems have no easy, quick solutions—at least that are apparent after just a few minutes of conversation. You may not have a clear idea what's at the root of the challenge.

By all means when you and the senior adult ministry can provide help, provide it. But don't jump the gun: be sure you understand situations first and offer solutions second. And here's good news: Becoming a better listener won't just make you a more effective volunteer—it will help you in other ways, too.

• **You'll be a better friend**

Not just with the seniors in your ministry but your friends, family and colleagues as well. As those people discover you're tracking with what they think and feel, they'll open up more. Mutual trust will grow. You'll have deeper, more meaningful relationships.

You'll be more successful at work—and life

Why? Because active listening cuts down on misunderstandings and demonstrates high emotional intelligence, which is directly correlated with success in teamwork situations. You'll be more productive because you'll be paying attention and more attune to the emotions of colleagues, better able to read what's happening around you.

• **You'll be happier**

Active listening skills can be deployed to resolve conflicts, grow closer to a spouse, engage strangers, and observe a world you may have previously ignored.

So practice listening. It will open doors and let you see through walls. In a world where confrontation is common and understanding increasingly rare, it's a superpower.

Though you'll have to provide your own cape.

CHAPTER 17

THE GRANDCHILD CONNECTION

*A*sk your congregation who considers themselves seniors and watch the hands slowly rise. Ask who's a grandparent and not only will far more hands shoot up, but pictures of grandkids will magically appear.

Many adults who don't want to identify as seniors are delighted to announce they're grandparents. In part that's because many grandparents truly aren't seniors.

"Most grandparents aren't senior adults," says Larry Fowler, founder of Legacy Coalition and arguably the grandfather of grandparent ministry. "The average age of a grandparent in the U.S. is 60 years old. The average age at which someone becomes a grandparent is 47 years of age."

With so many grandparents too young to slide into your senior adult ministry, why should you consider doing something special for grandparents? Because grandparents need to know how to intentionally help shape the faith of their grandkids, that's why. And because embracing that responsibility can provide an amazing sense of purpose in the lives of seniors in your ministry.

"If grandparents would really focus on their potential to impact their grandkids, it could be their most meaningful chapter of life," says Fowler.

If you choose to add "intentional grandparenting" to your roster of activities, Fowler suggests you take these six steps:

1. Recruit a core group of committed lay people.

This ministry will likely be its own organization rather than a part of your senior adult ministry because many participants won't be seniors.

2. Get pastoral sign-off.

You want this ministry to fit within the mission of your church and reflect your church's DNA. Your church leadership will help make sure that's the case.

3. Set the vision for spiritually intentional grandparenting.

The Bible has plenty to say about the role of grandparents in passing faith through the generations, but Fowler especially points at Deuteronomy 4:9.

4. Create a church culture that encourages grandparenting.

Preach about it. Add prayer for grandkids to the list of what groups normally pray about. Invite grandparents to be up front and central in baby dedications. Find practical congregational ways to communicate you believe grandparents have a biblical mandate to invest in the spiritual development of grandkids.

5. Equip grandparents. Give them support and practical ways to connect with their grandchildren, especially those who live remotely. One excellent source of ideas and training is Fowler's Legacy Coalition.

6. Host periodic special events for grandparents and grandkids, maybe a fun day of activities, perhaps a weekend camp.

If you choose to not launch a larger grandparent ministry, you can still talk about and pray for grandchildren in the context of your senior adult ministry. Doing so helps your seniors feel connected to some of the people they love most: their grandchildren.

For information on how to get access to the grandparenting resources offered by the Legacy Coalition, see Chapter 23.

CHAPTER 18

HONORING SENIORS

*M*iss Bonnie may be the only senior in the history of seniors who boycotted a "Honor Our Seniors" church service.

"You don't honor something just because it gets old," she says. "I've got a pie safe that belonged to my grandmother, and nobody honors it. Besides, I didn't feel all that honored when I went last year."

Bonnie is somewhere north of ninety and could charitably be called "feisty."

But she's right: the previous year at her church "honoring" service took the form of pausing to applaud the "senior saints" in attendance, asking those who could to stand. "That took some time," remembers Bonnie.

But nothing else in the service changed. A senior didn't deliver the sermon. No seniors were recruited to distribute communion. No senior sang a solo. It was business as usual other than briefly turning a spotlight on seniors and then switching the spotlight off for another year.

As a volunteer in senior adult ministry, you can honor the seniors in your care not just once a year, but every time you're with them.

Here's how:

It's honoring to be respected

- Ask permission before becoming overly familiar with a senior. It's "Mrs. Jennsen" until she gives you permission to call her Daisy.

- Encourage with specific rather than general compliments. Tell seniors what you appreciate about them and why. Be specific.
- Be kind and patient. It's respectful.
- Pray for and with seniors. Pausing to do that with individuals shows them you value them.
- Be as honest with seniors as you are with younger people. If Mr. Grimlett's snarky comments are a problem, take him aside and let him know. He doesn't get a pass because he's 80. Respect him enough to treat him like you'd treat anyone else.

It's honoring to be seen

- Learn the names of seniors in your ministry. If you're bad recalling names be sure at every meeting attendees wear nametags.
- Thank seniors for attending meetings. It probably took more effort than you know.
- Don't treat seniors as a "herd." They're individuals, each with a unique blend of strengths, weaknesses, and preferences. Discover those blends.
- Be curious about the backstories of your seniors. Where did they work? What experiences shaped them? Who are their family members?
- Acknowledge seniors publicly. Marilyn still remembers the boost she got when she walked into her exercise class and the leader smiled and called out, "Marilyn's here! Now it's a party!"

It's honoring to be heard

- Ask for seniors' stories, including stories about spouses who've died.

- Be interested when seniors talk. Listen carefully and ask follow-up questions.
- Ask seniors for their comments and advice.
- When you learn something from a senior, say so.
- Act on what seniors tell you. Even if you can't pull off what you're asked to do, it shows you were listening.

It's honoring to be celebrated, too

If you want to hold a Senior Sunday Service, go for it. But rather than have a sermon, give half a dozen seniors five minutes each to talk about one thing they've learned about God, or to share about a time they saw God come through. (May is a good time for that, by the way. I's Older Americans Month in the United States.)

CHAPTER 19

DO'S, DON'TS, AND TIPS TO TRY

*H*ere's some hard-won senior adult ministry wisdom from people who've been there:

- ## On handouts and other printed materials use 18-point type so it's easy for seniors with vision challenges to read the material. *This bullet point is set in 18-point type…see the difference?*

- Providing transportation in a senior-friendly vehicle greatly increases meeting attendance. Ask seniors to sit with new people each time.

- Do pray. Don't just talk about prayer, pray yourself, your ministry, and the seniors in it.

- Do have fun. If you're enjoying an activity, seniors are likely to come along for the ride.

- Do monitor competitive games carefully. Some of the most competitive people alive are seniors. And always review the rules of card games—many seniors grew up playing with variations of the official rules.

- Do add a few "Senior Parking Places" next to the handicap spots to make life easy for your mobility-challenged seniors who don't identify as "handicapped."
- Hearing aid squeals don't qualify as distractions. Do ignore them.
- Do shut down gossip as quickly as possible. It's toxic.
- Don't assume all seniors in your ministry have actually met or love Jesus. Share the gospel now and then and check to see if anyone wants to talk further.
- Do remember birthdays. (And just so you know, you have to special order "Happy 100!" cards in advance.)
- Do save space for seniors up front in the sanctuary so those with vision or hearing issues can more fully participate in services.
- On the church website and in printed materials do include photos of seniors, too. It sends a message.
- When you get pushback from seniors, assume positive intentions. Sometimes seniors think your ideas are dumb and sometimes they're right.
- If you'll be making nursing home or hospital visits and the smell bothers you, buy and carry a small vial of peppermint oil. A dash on your upper lip before your visit will cover most smells.
- Do find ways to give seniors significant jobs, not just the menial ones.
- Don't go it alone. Connect with others who work with seniors (churches, nursing homes, assisted

living facilities) and see what you can learn. Keep learning.

- Don't call on seniors to read in public without checking first.
- Do smile a lot. Seniors generally see far too few smiles.
- Don't disrespect younger generations or let seniors do it at your meetings. They're not the enemy.
- Do welcome seniors as they are but don't let them stay there. Expect them to deepen in discipleship and provide resources to help that happen. You're not just keeping seniors safe until Jesus comes to collect them.
- Do proceed with a meeting even if only a couple seniors attend. It communicates you value attendees.
- Do lobby hard for raised toilet seats. Seniors with arthritis will thank you. And lots of accessibility hardware in toilet stalls as well.
- Do delegate whenever you can to seniors. It builds their investment in the ministry. Refreshments, announcements, planning—all can be delegated.
- Do let seniors know you're available. (But give seniors your cell phone number "just in case" only if you're ready to get calls.)
- Do speak simply and clearly. Enunciate the way your mother always hoped you would.
- Do hand out sincere compliments by the bucketload.
- Be careful about cliques forming in your ministry. It's good seniors have friends, but be mindful new

people need a welcoming place to land when they come.

- Do keep confidences unless someone threatens to harm another or himself, or there's something illegal going on. Find out who you need to report to now, before there's a problem.
- Don't expect every senior to like you or want to be your friend.
- Do set and maintain boundaries. Hold time for your family, friends, and interests. It's okay to say, "no."
- Do try meeting in the homes of some of your seniors. Let them have the joy of hospitality.
- Do get to know the families of your seniors. Give them opportunities to talk about their kids, grandkids, and great grandkids. Pets, too.
- Never pick out a curriculum without having a few seniors vet it.
- Don't be afraid to use the web and social media platforms with seniors. Some seniors won't use, them but many will. These are the people who *invented* the internet, you know.
- Do borrow a friendly dog for a little pet therapy at your next meeting. Announce you're doing it, though—you don't want an unexpected allergic reaction.
- Don't try the same thing with a cat. Truly. Trust us on this.
- Less is more. Experiment with lots of programs but if something isn't working, cut it.
- Do keep meeting places safe for walkers and canes. Clear away clutter.

- Do put a couple youth group kids in wheelchairs and let them test whether your facility is truly wheelchair friendly. Ask them to make notes of where they met obstacles. Monitor the experiments!
- Do be yourself—everyone else is already taken anyway.

CHAPTER 20

IN CASE OF EMERGENCY

*O*lder seniors are a vulnerable population, which means certain issues can quickly become emergencies in their lives. As a volunteer in your senior adult ministry, be ready to respond should you encounter:

Health Crises

Basic first aid training is a must for volunteers like you. Contact your local Red Cross office to find out what training is available and at minimum become certified in CPR. Carry a basic first aid kit when your group of seniors goes on outings, too.

The National Council on Aging (NCOA) estimates about 80 percent of seniors have at least one chronic disease and one in four falls each year. Learn now how to respond if a senior experiences a health crisis or takes a tumble.[7]

And a question for your leaders: Should a signed release be required for participants to go on outings and field trips?

Elder Abuse

NCOA reports that about one in 10 Americans aged 60 or older have suffered some type of elder abuse—an inappropriate act that harms an older person physically, emotionally, or financially.[8]

---

7   https://www.ncoa.org/article/get-the-facts-on-healthy-aging

8   https://www.nursinghomeabusecenter.com/elder-abuse/signs

Symptoms of elder abuse include injuries such as bruises, cuts, or broken bones; poor hygiene; malnourishment or weight loss; unexplained loss of money; anxiety, depression, confusion; or withdrawal from family members or friends.

If you suspect elder abuse notify your ministry leader immediately. If you *are* the ministry leader, report your suspicions to the police. You may not be a mandatory reporter, but you are committed to act in the best interest of your seniors.

Cognitive Health Crises

With advancing age comes an increased chance of dementia, including Alzheimer's disease. It takes a professional to diagnose dementia, but early symptoms include significant memory loss, difficulty in completing familiar tasks, and confusion regarding time or place.

If you notice these issues arising in a senior's life, don't offer an uninformed diagnosis. But do make a mental note to check with a person in that senior's life who might be able to tell you if their senior has a cognitive health issue.

That's something you'll want to know.

Crises of Faith

Belief that physical death isn't the final word gets a fresh analysis from seniors who've attended three funerals in the past month. Is what they accepted easily at 20 still reasonable now that they're 78? What do they really believe? How should they live if their faith is faltering?

Bottom line: you can't prove what happens five minutes after someone dies, but you can offer reassurance by sharing Bible passages (Chapter 14), listening attentively, and reminding seniors of God's faithfulness in the past.

A hint: gently probe whether the issue is a fear God isn't there, a fear the senior hasn't earned a place in heaven, or a fear of the process of dying. If it's the first issue, remind the senior of God's faithfulness. If it's the second, focus on grace. If it's the third, sympathize—we'll all face it.

It's also always a good idea as a senior adult ministry volunteer to know who on the team or in the church is trained for medical emergencies, and to keep a list of local emergency services contact numbers handy in your phone.

CHAPTER 21

JOB DESCRIPTION TEMPLATE

*D*o you really need a detailed job description?

No. Most volunteers do ministry without one. However, if you know what your leaders expect of you, you're better able to do it. You can make decisions about which opportunities to pursue and which to let sail on past.

You'll know where you're headed and why.

A job description can help you in all those areas, but we can't show you one. The reason is that each senior adult ministry looks different. So rather than guess how yours looks, sit with your leader and together fill in the details in the job description template that follows. And if your leader has already given you a job description, give that leader a hug.

Job Description: [Your official title]

Church Mission and Vision Statements: [add below]

Mission and/or Vision Statements for the Senior Adult Ministry: [add below, checking to see that what's there is in alignment with your church's larger mission and vision]

Summary of This Job: [In a nutshell, what you're expected to do]

Responsibilities: [the *specifics* of what you're expected to do]

•

•

•

•

This Position Reports To: [who to call when you have questions or concerns and how to reach that person]

There it is. It's that simple. The real benefit isn't just that you have a job description, but that you and your leader talked it through together. You're now on the same page and heading the same direction.

CHAPTER 22

DISCUSSION QUESTIONS

*J*f you're going through this book with other volunteers, these questions can help you apply each chapter. And if you're reading this on your own, the questions are equally valuable. Jot down your responses and see what your answers tell you.

1. What the Bible Says About Senior Adult Ministry

What are three words that describe your honest feelings about seniors? What do those words tell you?

- In what ways is your church providing for elderly people who need support?

2. Why Your Senior Adult Ministry Matters

- Which of the four reasons presented about why you ministry matters seems most important to you? What's a reason you'd add to the list?
- Where—if anywhere—do you see ageism in your church?

3. Qualities of an Effective Senior Adult Ministry

- What are three examples of how your ministry is Jesus-centered?
- How are you currently promoting spiritual growth in seniors? What would you like to add to what you're doing?

4. Models of Senior Adult Ministry

- Are you currently ministering to seniors, with seniors, or both?
- Which of the models presented is like what you're doing now? Which, if any, would you like to incorporate?

5. Sorting Out the Seniors

- Who do you consider a "senior" in your church? If there's an age you've selected, why did you pick that age?
- When you pray for your seniors, what do you pray?

6. Qualities of Effective Senior Adult Ministry Volunteers

- Which of these qualities reminds you of you?
- Which of these qualities sounds least like you—at present, anyway?

7. 15 Ideas to Energize Sunday School for Seniors

- How are you encouraging fellowship in your adult Sunday school?
- Which of these 15 ideas sound like something to give a try?

8. Guiding Seniors Through Change

- Tell about a time someone assumed they knew how you feel? What was that like for you?
- What are some changes your seniors would like to make?

9. In-Reach to Seniors

- Which of these ways to connect with seniors is working best for you?
- Which idea would you like to try?

10. Outreach to Seniors

- What's your answer to the WIIFM question regarding your ministry?
- If you could add one more outreach approach, which would you pick?

11. Engaging Go-Go's, Slow-Go's, and No-Go's

- What's your mixture of Go-Go's, Slow-Go's, and No-Go's? How is impacting the activities you do in your ministry? What if you had something for everyone?
- Which of these dozens of ideas would you like to try?

12. 13 Senior-Sized Service Projects

- Which service idea you've not tried do you want to try? Why that one?
- How does the idea of intergenerational service projects strike you?

13. Short-Term Mission Opportunities

- How well have seniors participated in short term missions in the past? What do you think would increase participation?
- Which of these ideas would you like to explore?

14. Scriptures That Speak to the Needs of Seniors

- How will you keep this list handy so you have it when you need it? (Spoiler Alert: Photocopy the list and keep the copy in your Bible.)

- Which of these passages speaks especially loudly to you today?

15. Helping Seniors Deal With Loneliness and Grief
- Who will you put on your list of referrals?
- How prevalent is loneliness among your seniors? Why do you answer as you do?

16. Becoming a Listening Place
- What sort of listener are you? Give an example of why you answer as you do.
- Which of the listening exercises will you do first?

17. The Grandchild Connection
- What would be the value of a grandparent ministry in your church? To your seniors?
- How will you use the grandchild connection in your ministry to seniors even if your church doesn't embrace a grandparent ministry?

18. Honoring the Elderly
- Which of the specific suggestions for respecting, seeing, and hearing seniors strikes you as something to start doing with more intentionality?
- Which of the specific suggestions do you think you already do well?

19. Do's, Don'ts, and Tips to Try
- What's one "don't" you should start "don't-ing?"
- And one "do" you should start "doing?"

CHAPTER 23

RECOMMENDED RESOURCES

Caring Congregation Ministry Implementation Guide by Karen Lampe and Melissa Gepford (Abingdon Press, 2021)

Caring Congregation Ministry Care Minister's Manual by Karen Lampe (Abingdon Press, 2021)

Senior Adult Ministry in the 21st Century by Dr. David P. Gallagher (Group Publishing, 2002)

An Age of Opportunity: Intentional Older Adult Ministry by Richard H. Gentzler, Jr. (Discipleship Resources, 2018)

Senior Adult Ministries: Taking Your Senior Adult Ministries to the Next Level by Ray Jones (Available on Amazon, 2019)

Baby Boomers and Beyond: Tapping the Ministry Talents and Passions of Adults over 50 by Amy Hanson (Jossey-Bass, 2010)

Legacy Coalition podcast: legacycoalition.com/podcast

Legacy Coalition resources: legacycoalition.com/resources

Legacy Coalition weekly webinar: legacycoalition.com/grand-Monday-nights

ABOUT THE CONTRIBUTORS

There are people cheering you on as you embrace senior adult ministry. Among them are these generous people who contributed their wisdom and insights to this book:

Pat Baker has served two congregations as Director of Older Adult Ministry and is a founding member of the National Presbyterian Older Adult Ministry Network. She served as Director of Health and Human Services in Gwinnett County, Georgia, and has consulted with AARP, The Rosalynn Carter Institute for Caregiving, the Alzheimer's Association, and now, you!

Jess Welch serves as the Connection and Care Assistant at Cookeville First United Methodist Church in Cookeville, Tennessee. That makes her mission control when it comes to linking hurting parishioners with ministries that can meet their needs. Jess is grateful her church has an established ministry for church members 55 years of age and older.

Dan Johnson is chaplain of the Great Lakes Christian Home in Holt, Michigan. After serving for years in a local church Dan's ministry is now all-seniors, all the time, including in his off hours. That's because Dan is a senior himself.

Larry Fowler is an author, speaker, and the founder of the Legacy Coalition. His 40+ years in ministry included time serving as a youth pastor, an Awana missionary and trainer, and coach in both children's ministry and grandparenting.

Special thanks to these ministry workers and seniors whose insights and stories contributed so much: Doug, Carol, Dick and Karen, mark, Dale, Nancy, Judy, Tricia, Mike, Cindy, Greg, and Bonnie. *(Due to the personal nature of their stories, some names of people in this list have been changed to ensure confidentiality.)*

Author

Mikal Keefer has published more than 40 books for children, youth, and adults, as well as writing for a wide array of magazines and curricula. He's a senior himself and just got the news: hearing aids are in his future.

General Editor

Matt Lockhart has spent more than twenty-five years in a variety of editorial and leadership roles in Christian publishing at Serendipity House, Group, and Standard/David C Cook. And no, he's not yet a senior, but don't hold that against him.

Names   Phone and Email

_____   _____

_____   _____

_____   _____

_____   _____

_____   _____

_____   _____

_____   _____

_____   _____

SENIOR ADULT MINISTRY TEAM CONTACT INFORMATION

Names   Phone and Email

_____   _____

_____   _____

_____   _____

_____   _____

_____   _____

_____   _____

_____   _____

_____   _____

_____   _____

SENIOR ADULT MINISTRY TEAM NOTES

How Can a Prayer Ministry Transform Your Church?

Whether you are part of your church's prayer ministry, or thinking about starting or joining a prayer ministry team, the *Prayer Ministry Volunteer Handbook* is for you!

We are often very quick to say we will pray for someone when we hear they are going through tough times, but do we actually follow through with our promise to pray for them? How many times do we turn to prayer only in times of crisis, as a last resort, or simply to ask things of God?

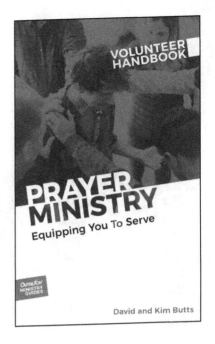

We need to make prayer the first course of action, guiding all of our life decisions. We must challenge ourselves to move beyond the dinnertime and bedtime prayers and progress to a thoughtful conversation with Christ.

Join authors David and Kim Butts as they explore how a well-equipped church prayer ministry team can serve as a model and an encouragement to support the members of the congregation, and even the pastoral staff, in their prayer journeys. Discover how you can make your church a house of prayer for all believers.

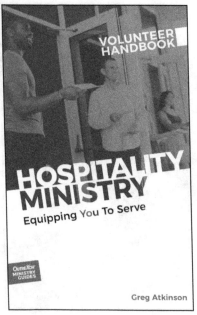

Be Our Guest

Whether you are a volunteer in your church's guest services ministry, or thinking about serving alongside ushers, greeters, welcome desk hosts, and parking lot attendants at your church, the *Hospitality Ministry Volunteer Handbook* is for you!

How does a member of community see your church? When they hear your church's name, what is their initial reaction? We want any individual who steps foot onto our church campus to immediately feel Christ's love through our actions toward them—the question is, are we doing a good job at accomplishing that mission?

We might not think of customer service and church hospitality in the same vein, but this book shows how a service mentality can make life-changing first impressions on newcomers. It's filled with specific, practical strategies and tools to help the hospitality ministry team show the love of Christ to every visitor.

Join author Greg Atkinson as he helps identify ways your church can increase its hospitality to the community around you, and, ultimately, reach those people for the Kingdom of God.

Practical Outreach Ideas and Ministry Tools

Never has there been a greater need to share the good news of God's love with those in our communities. This compact handbook shows how individual Christians and ministry teams can share the gospel by reaching out to and serving others.

Featuring 121 outreach ideas, this book helps to equip ministry teams with practical tools to serve families, children, youth, seniors, first responders, the oppressed and under resourced, millennials, single parents, local schools and businesses and more!

Designed for ministry volunteers, the book is a compact handbook of outreach ministry helps, which in addition to the dozens of outreach ideas also include outreach Scriptures and prayers, ways to share your faith, team discussion questions and recommended outreach ministries and resources.

This helpful little book is a great resource for equipping outreach ministry volunteers to serve others and to share the good news!

Equipping Children's Ministry Volunteers

Whether you are part of your church's children's ministry, or thinking about serving in children's ministry, the *Children's Ministry Volunteer Handbook* is for you!

Too often, people view children's ministry as a place to drop off the kids so the adults can listen to the sermon, uninterrupted. They fail to see the power and potential of children's ministry.

In Matthew 19:13-14, Jesus said, "Let the little children come to me, and do not hinder them, for the kingdom of heaven belongs to such as these." While we may see the naivete of children as a detriment, Jesus sees it as a strength—there is beauty in the simplicity of the gospel. Investing in children's ministry is a worthwhile and crucial part of the church.

This practical handbook features insights from six authors, all experts in the field of children's ministry, with over 100 years of combined experience. They will help guide you through the challenges and joys of children's ministry—and how it is vital to the Kingdom of God.

VOLUNTEER HANDBOOK

CARE AND VISITATION MINISTRY

Equipping You To Serve

OUTREACH MINISTRY GUIDES

Mikal Keefer

Talk About More Than the Weather

You've driven to the hospital and stand outside a patient's room, ready to knock and ask permission to enter. But then what? How do you make a visit that actually matters?

Here are hundreds of practical tips gleaned from the experience of veteran visitors—chaplains, pastors, and volunteers who've made thousands of visits in hospitals, nursing care facilities, rehab centers, homes, hospice centers, even prisons.

They share what to do, what not to do, and how to connect in caring, compassionate ways with people who may be experiencing the worst days of their lives.

Discover how to make visits that matter—that literally change lives—as you carry the love of Jesus to those who are sick, lonely, or simply curious about the Kingdom.

VOLUNTEER HANDBOOK

SMALL GROUP MINISTRY

Equipping You To Serve

OUTREACH MINISTRY GUIDES

Mikal Keefer

Equip Small Group Leaders to Lead Well

Your church's small group ministry is where faith can get real. Where masks can slide off and honest struggles and doubts surface.

Maybe. It all depends on the leaders of your groups.

Give your leaders the training they need to take group members deeper. To create group cultures that encourage transparency. To cope with questions, deal with doubts, and make disciples.

This book offers your team a lifetime of easy-to-read, easy-to-remember advice from experienced small group ministry leaders. They share what they've learned, what they wish they'd known earlier, and dozens of proven practical tips that will aid in developing healthy small groups in your church.

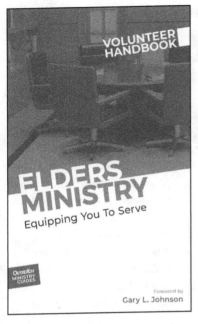

VOLUNTEER
HANDBOOK

ELDERS MINISTRY
Equipping You To Serve

OUTREACH
MINISTRY
GUIDES

Foreword by
Gary L. Johnson

Biblical Guidance and Practical Advice for Church Elders and Prospective Elders

Equip church elders to lead well. More than better methods, the church today needs better leaders. But too often we recruit these leaders (the New Testament calls them *elders*) without equipping them for their vital task. This practical handbook presents the need, lifts up the Bible's vision for elder ministry, and provides a wealth of practical how-to training to help elders provide the spiritual leadership that can't come from anyone else. Elder teams will build unity and confidence as they discuss it together.

Written by the ministry founders and leaders of e2: effective elders, content is based on decades of local-church experience and interaction with everyday elders in hundreds of congregations.

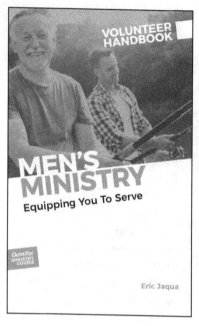

A men's ministry that guys will look forward to being a part of!

Every church wants to actively engage and grow men—but most men's ministries have a hard time getting guys in the door. This wildly practical ministry handbook equips men's ministry volunteers and their leaders with proven suggestions for building a program that's magnetic to men.

Give your ministry team the tools, tips, and training they need to help develop the trust and accountability between men which leads to deep, lasting spiritual growth.

Included within this helpful men's ministry guide:
- Practical ways to get men into the Word
- Guidance for effective men's group meetings
- Dozens of ideas for serving together, fostering accountability, strengthening family connections, and more!

CPSIA information can be obtained
at www.ICGtesting.com
Printed in the USA
LVHW111627090922
727998LV00004B/731